CREATING UNLIMITED OPTIONS FOR AGING

The Path Forward

by Joseph Carella

Cover design: Karen Ancas
Editor: Stephanie Schorow

Contents

Preface

In writing the first edition of *Unlimited Options for Aging* back in 1995 and now with *Creating Unlimited Options for Aging*, Joe Carella shares a compassion for elder care that comes from personal experience and over 25 years as the Executive Director of the Scandinavian Charitable Society of Greater Boston. In these books, Joe shares the experience from which we can see the real empathy and the vision he pursues each day to help improve the dignity with which people live in their elder years.

I met Joe in 1990 when my grandmother came to reside in what was then called the Swedish Home in which Joe was the director. In 1995 I read the first edition of *Unlimited Options for Aging*. The vision Joe articulated compelled me to accept the offer to join the Board of Directors of the Scandinavian Charitable Society, which today oversees the Scandinavian Living Center (SLC), an assisted living community with 40 apartments, and the Scandinavian Cultural Center (SCC). These institutions are physically and operationally integrated in connecting the broader community with SLC residents. Under Joe's leadership, the creation and operation of the SLC and the SCC reflect the vision and concepts of elder living that are articulated in this book.

While I do not have much experience with elder living enterprises outside the SLC, I, unfortunately, have seen enough to have a visceral experience of gross lapses in providing dignified care in an institutional setting. The four principles of *Creating Unlimited Options for Aging* describe a way of living that I was happy to see my grandmother enjoy and a reality I hope my parents and someday my wife and I will be fortunate to experience in our elder years.

Joe presents what he calls simple concepts: encouraging community-centered living, offering a welcoming residential reality versus an institutional reality, encouraging autonomy, and maintaining and developing one's lifestyle. I agree they are simple concepts as Joe notes, but they are, nonetheless, profound. This book presents current research with strong insight and clarity. The call to advance these principles is both relevant and, unfortunately for far too many, urgent. While we see more residential options for elders with a la carte services in the U.S. marketplace, this is a market segment that is not affordable by many and is most commonly lacking connection with the broader community.

I believe that the principles in *Creating Unlimited Options for Aging* can be appreciated from any worldview and applied in any cultural context. I can attest that the fundamentals that Joe identified in his Scandinavian research are today providing a rich way of life for the residents of the SLC, their families and the community of West Newton, Massachusetts.

In Pope Francis' encyclical, "Laudato Si; On Care for Our Common Home," a central theme is "integral ecology" which the Pope defines as: "Everything is connected. Concern for the environment thus needs to be joined to a sincere love for our fellow human beings and unwavering commitment to resolving the problems of society." I see Joe presenting us with "integral elder living." He is encouraging and facilitating connection with the elders in our communities with a sincere love for each other. Joe has held an unwavering commitment to the dignity of elders that is reflected in the pages of this book.

The statistics on the growing need are striking. The percentage of people in the United States over the age of 65 climbed from 4 percent in 1900 to 13 percent in 2010 and is predicted to climb to 20 percent by 2050[1]. Globally, it is expected to climb from 8 percent in 2010 to 16 percent by 2050.[2]

I believe the community-centered approach Joe shares could help meet the common needs of an aging population in any societal context. The elder quality-of-life would be the better for it and all members of society enriched.

David Wilson, MA, is a health economic and outcome researcher who heads Evidence Development Strategy Consulting. He has held positions within medical device, biopharmaceutical, consulting, and contract research organizations companies as well as academia. Mr. Wilson currently sits on the boards of Lexington Christian Academy and the Scandinavian Charitable Society of Greater Boston.

Acknowledgement

Many thanks to Fran Dragon, an angel, who continues to inspire improvement and better human connection…

In loving memory of my mother,

Carmela (Millie) Galluzzo Carella

04-03-1927 to 10-25-2017

Introduction

*Humility is when you understand
that you know less than others.
Confidence is when you understand
what little you know is right.*

In 1995, I wrote a book called *Unlimited Options for Aging* in reaction to an outdated elder housing environment. I wanted to present an innovative, life-enhancing alternative fueled by insight gained from my observations and experiences. *Unlimited Options for Aging* outlined an alternative to the institution-like housing environment in the United States.

In my book, I outlined three principles for elder housing:

1) Elder housing should create a positive residential reality.
2) Housing should allow residents to maintain their lifestyle.
3) Housing should encourage antonomy.

1

Six years later, my vision became a reality. In 2001, we dedicated the Scandinavian Living Center (SLC), a community developed and sustained on *Unlimited Options for Aging's* core three principles. Now, 17 years later, I still believe these principles can guide any senior living option and will never become outdated. They are easy to implement and are the bedrock of good design and development.

So why write a new book now? The answer is simple. There is ANOTHER principle, to which I only alluded in the first book, that I now believe needs to be the most important consideration when creating a life-enhancing living environment: the principle of community-centered living.

What is community-centered living?

- Community-centered living means encouraging everyone to interact without feeling they are outsiders. Community-centered living breaks down the walls of separation that lead to isolated living, but more importantly, it allows those who are limited physically or mentally to stay naturally connected to the surrounding world. This is possible by encouraging a variety of many different and ongoing opportunities for "ageless" human connections. Finding ways to bring neighbors and friends of all ages together is an important element of community-centered-living.
- Community-centered living encourages people to continue life's journey in a supportive environment, empowering them to choose how they want to share interests and values. It does this by creating a welcoming residential setting that is not only safe, but offers an atmosphere and environment that is welcoming to all ages. Community-centered living is proactive in constantly creating different opportunities for people

to come together through shared interest, choice or lifestyle.

- Community-centered living creates opportunities for human connections and allows individuals of all ages to choose how they want to participate in these connections. Community-centered living respects seniors as integral members of the community and by doing so, it allows them to pass on their special inheritance.

In introducing this important principle of "community-centered living," I hope to demonstrate why it should be incorporated into all types of living environments. Without community-centered living, a perfectly designed and developed housing project can be engulfed by an institutional atmosphere. No matter how big, how beautiful, or how much of a county-club-like atmosphere, the project will become isolating and institution-like unless a concerted effort is made toward developing community-centered living. Using this principle connects generations. By ignoring it, every generation loses out. Community-centered living must be the basic principle used to create unlimited options for aging.

These four principles are not stand-alone concepts. They are more like ingredients to be mixed, intertwined, and connected throughout the design and development of any type of housing community. I have learned over the years that community-centered living is the most difficult of the four principles to comprehend and develop. For our purposes, when we speak about community, we are including individuals living inside a housing structure as well as their neighbors of all ages in the surrounding city or town. Housing units include all types of living arrangements from independent apartments and homes to assisted living facilities and nursing homes.

This new book, *Creating Unlimited Options for Aging*, lays out the rationale for community-centered living, explores its ramifications, and examines how it can be instituted on a worldwide, multi-cultural basis. To understand the deep implications of this principle, I need to explain how my own life experience shaped its creation as well as the other core values of *Unlimited Options for Aging*. So, I begin this book with my personal journey and how crucial events in my life and key people shaped my vision. The journey begins, as do so many, in my childhood. But it begins with a profound tragedy.

CHAPTER 1

A Personal Journey

"Without everyone, we are no one."

Finn Kristoan Hannestad

Growing up in Arlington, Massachusetts, in the 1960s, I knew every family on my block — and there were more than 30 children, eight young couples and a dozen elders. The most important people to me were the family across the street. Dorothy and Ralph Guanci had seven kids — and there were six kids in my family. My good friend Joe Guanci was, like me, the youngest sibling. My oldest brother Charlie was a paperboy like Jerry, the oldest Guanci boy. Indeed, it seemed each Guanci child lined up some way with a child in our family. We were always in each other's home. The Guanci connection taught me about friendship. It also taught me about tragedy.

Shortly after Joe was born, Dorothy Guanci passed away. The father's mother moved in to assist her son Ralph rear the seven children. Mrs. Guanci had already raised six children and had recently lost her husband. Now, she was called upon to help raise another large family. Eventually, the neighborhood became part of the supporting fabric that helped Mrs. Guanci care for her family. We felt like we were part of each other's lives.

Everyone in the neighborhood seemed to know each other well and we all talked — young or old — when we met on the street. For example, knowing that I was not fond of potatoes, one of my older neighbors, Pop Lionetta, shared a simple and tasty potato recipe that I have never forgotten. I have shared it with my own family, and in a small way his legacy, this connection, continues. I often ran errands for Mrs. Stanley, another elder, and we had wonderful conversations. Once, she saw that I was a little upset with my older siblings, and she offered a bit of wisdom. She told me that as the youngest in my family, I had the opportunity to observe the mistakes of my five older brothers and sisters and that through these observations I would find a way to avoid similar missteps. I did not realize it at the time, but this bit of wisdom stuck with me for years.

I remember the time when my brother Bob begged our grandmother to visit Mrs. Guanci to talk her out of not punishing her grandson — his best friend Peter — so he could play with him outside. After several minutes of a heated Italian discussion between the two elders, Peter was released and out he came with a big smile on his face. Both grandmothers would cross the street to visit each other and share their stories and in some cases, help each other out. Years later Mrs. Guanci would find time to visit my grandmother and assist her with changing her dressings as she was recovering from medical treatments. She continued to help until my grandmother passed from cancer.

One summer the oldest boys from both families, Charlie and Jerry, both paperboys, won a contest held by the local newspaper; the top prize was a trip to New York City for a fun-filled weekend. The boys could barely contain their excitement. Charlie and Jerry just completed eighth grade, were the best of friends, and were naturally overjoyed about the opportunity to visit New York City. On the day of the trip, both boys had finished packing and just needed to deliver the final Friday newspapers before embarking on what seemed to both a trip of a lifetime. With great anticipation, they both went off to complete this last responsibility. Two hours later, Charlie returned from his paper route to discover that Jerry had been hit by a truck and killed.

Once again, the Guanci family experienced another unthinkable tragedy. Yet the family and the neighborhood became closer; together we sought a way to help them live through this horrible accident and find a way to happiness again. Two years later, the father suddenly passed away. A young family, once so full of life and enthusiasm, now found themselves faced with no parents, the loss of the oldest child and a grandmother who had been asked to take on the responsibility of rearing six young children. Overnight it seemed that our families came together and that our family had enlarged by six children plus a grandmother.

Amazingly, the Guanci family not only overcame these tragedies, with their grandmother's leadership, they moved forward in life. Growing up, my best friend Joe was a model of natural kindness, but more importantly he, like most of his siblings, retained his funny bone and would instill in me the importance of laughing at many moments in life. Often, I would find myself in tears from laughing so hard - Joe could make me laugh at almost anything in life. Through this family's tragedies and their examples, I would come to embrace the importance of moving through difficult times with a conquering spirit, a kind smile, and a humorous attitude. Through Mrs. Guanci, we would learn that in dealing with setbacks or terrible lows, life must carry on and you are never too busy to be part of helping others.

My neighborhood represented a small village of people who came together to help each other. The village movement created several years ago has its origins from this type of neighborhood. Unlike today's village movement in which middle-age and older adults volunteer to help each other out, a more natural village is made up of all ages, like my street in Arlington. My neighborhood and my experiences there, particularly with the Guanci family, evolved into my commitment to the idea of community-centered living.

In remembering my Arlington neighbors, I have come to realize that ordinary simple connections are important ingredients for the growth and the quality of life for all generations. Observations and human interactions can be random and seemingly uneventful. However, over a lifetime, some of these unplanned connections can lead to life-changing decisions.

As I grew up and attended high school I came to experience something that Robert H. Hopkins describes in his book *There Are No Accidents:* several synchronistic events that would impact my understanding of aging. Synchronicity is a term coined by C. G. Jung, to indicate meaningful coincidences that may seem meaningless to one party, but have a profound effect on the other person. In other words, a human connection between two people may be random and forgettable by one, but could change the course of the other person's life. Hopkins says that these moments are unplanned, random, and may lead to a deep emotional experience, and that the effect occurs during a transitional phase leading to some type of turning point.[3]

One of these synchronistic events occurred during my high school years. I had an athletic injury that required surgery and recuperation in a hospital in 1979. During the hospital admission process, I was told that the pediatric ward was closed and that I would need to be transferred to the geriatric ward. I did not know then what the word "geriatric" meant. Instead of recovering among my peers, I was placed in a room with two elderly men. One had advanced dementia, and the other was silently contemplating the future loss of his gangrenous legs. As a physically fit, upbeat teenager, there was no way I could have anticipated the way the experience would profoundly affect me. My main concerns were sports, dating, school — the usual things. But I suddenly was taken out of my element and put into a situation where I would live as an "elderly" person and be forced to observe things from that perspective.

I spoke to one of my roommates while he was eating, not realizing initially that he had advanced dementia. As I talked to him, he continued to shovel food into his mouth. His only interaction with others occurred when he was eating. Nurses would present him with food and he would devour it. They would later return, wipe his mouth, and remove his dishes. He had no other connection to the real world. He just sat and stared.

My other roommate, Frankie, was a quiet and private man. At first, I did not know that his legs were gangrenous, but I quickly discovered what this meant. One evening he dismissed his wife, daughter and doctor from the room after they had asked for his consent to amputate his legs. When they had gone, he spoke to me for the first time, saying, "What am I to do?" I thought to myself, "What can I say to help comfort an elder who is so much older and wiser than I?"

Frankie's legs eventually were amputated. This was not the only loss I experienced during my stay. Unbeknownst to me, a man who had become somewhat of a second father, died in the same hospital. I was informed about his death by a candy striper friend. Unintentionally, she carelessly told me, "Oh, by the way, John died. You knew that, right?" I did not know and I was devastated. I felt I had lost control of my life. I could not change what was happening. I had met a man who had lost his mind, another who had lost his legs. And, now a man, so important to me, had lost his life.

I now realize that, in that geriatric ward everyone's options were limited. Frankie saw no other option available to him. The man with advanced dementia could not communicate with those around him. From my bed, I could see into the hallway where older patients, tied to their wheelchairs, were sometimes injected with medication to keep them calm.

I, too, now experienced limitations, and not just physical limitations. I found that my most profound limits were psychological. My power of choice had been taken away. I could not leave my bed; I could not leave my room. I could not withdraw from the emotionally wrenching realities of my roommates. I was forced to witness their pain and suffering as well as the grief of their families.

Yet, I was experiencing emotions that would help me mature. The "inconvenience" of my right knee injury, my immobility, and the possibility of not being able to play football, began to seem unimportant. How could I lie there, feeling sorry for myself, while my roommates were dealing with profound and devastating changes? I began to closely observe how they were treated. By the fourth day of my hospitalization, as my sister would later tell me, I began to exhibit the behavior of an "elderly" person. I remember that my mind wandered as I felt helpless and out of control. The effects of this brief experience — four days and four nights — were profound. My blood pressure rose from a normal 120/80 to 230/180. With sweat rolling down my face, I begged the director of nursing, who ironically was retiring that week, to move me out of the geriatric ward. It occurred to me later that the director's final act, before she walked into retirement and unknown aging options, was relocating me to the pediatric ward.

It turned out that there had been a mistake. The pediatric ward had been open all week. How could this happen, I wondered. My move to the pediatric unit seemed to remove my limitations, and my mental torment eased. My roommates' options remained limited. Frankie never recovered from his amputations even though he tried to adjust. He died three weeks later having lost the will to live. Four days later after my move to the pediatric ward, I left the hospital profoundly changed, energized, and with new direction in life. This emotional experience connecting with these elders now focused my perspective and intensified my energy and observational ability moving forward. I remember looking out the window of the pediatric ward and seeing a hearse pull up to the morgue entrance. This seemed to symbolize the death of my innocence.

But now I was interested in issues of elder care and very soon I was aware that this could be my calling in life. As our family helped the Guanci family, maybe I could help elderly folks with their lives — even people like Frank and my roommate with dementia. However, I had no idea where to begin. I started to volunteer at nursing homes, and I continued to interact with elders through my part-time job at a local grocery store where I delivered groceries. I was also invited by friends to volunteer at a local housing community for the mentally challenged. Each week we would visit the housing units and on Sunday bring some of the clients to the local church on campus. On one of those Sundays, I had a random discussion with the Catholic priest in charge. Hearing my interests, he suggested a strategy in which I would study an aspect of healthcare at a local university that offered meaningful cooperative work opportunities throughout the course of a five-year program. However, he also recommended that I needed to stay away from all aspects of elder care at first. This did not make sense to me, but he went on to explain that I would be involved in elder care for most of my adult life and now was the time to experience other opportunities and adventures before I embarked on my long-term goals. I remember asking when will I be ready? He just told me that I would know when the time came to start my elder care training.

So now I had a focus. During the next few years, I studied for my undergraduate degree at Northeastern University and I worked for several different companies. In 1984, I travelled to Haiti and I spent months traveling cross-country in the United States. During this time, I was on top of my game, and I seemed to always capture the best co-op jobs and opportunities that came my way.

However, life never moves in a straight line. Even as I began my college studies, I learned I had a genetic kidney disorder. I was told the disease would eventually lead to kidney failure and I would need a kidney. As it turned out, two of my cousins had the same disorder and had received kidneys from their siblings. At first, I was in denial; I thought I could outrun or out exercise this condition. I was too healthy and strong not to believe that I would be the exception. Having this cloud over me was enough to push me to excel and dive into as many different experiences that opportunity would bring my way. I eventually graduated college and later that summer in 1985, I packed my bags and embarked on a cross-country trip that would keep me away from home until the end of

November. As I returned for Thanksgiving, I told my family I was moving to Arizona; I had rented an apartment starting December while I was traveling through Phoenix that fall.

Looking back on it now, this spontaneity seemed normal; it was something you do in your twenties. But I now know that it was my way to get away from everyone as I continued to deal with my kidney problem. During the next year and a half in Phoenix, I would indeed experience kidney failure. As a physician explained, I would continue to decline up until I was "close to my death bed" and only then, would they make the decision to transplant a kidney. Fortunately, I had a perfect match with my sister and knew that it was just going to be a waiting game. I had no idea how long this process would take, but knew I needed to pay attention to this experience. Ironically, having been told to stay away from elder care, my physical body seemed to be aging; I was losing weight and physically deteriorating. My energy declined to the point that I needed to sleep constantly; I became weaker, colder and lighter as my appetite slipped away. I eventually returned home in 1987 weighing 120 pounds, down from a high of 180. Within weeks I was in a Boston hospital preparing for surgery.

As I lay in the pre-op ward waiting to have my kidney transplant the next day, I felt as if my world was collapsing around me. I did not understand why this had happened to me. In short, I was feeling sorry for myself.

In my hospital room were three men; two of them would leave a lasting impression on me. My roommate next to me had suffered an accident years earlier and was now paralyzed. As he told me about his story and the adventures of his life, it became apparent that I needed to stop feeling sorry for myself. As he would say to me with a kind smile, "Take what you have and make the best of it." Listening to this roommate, I could not stop noticing the man across the room; he was excited because he was about to receive a kidney from his identical twin and the match was the best you could get when it comes to organ implants. In other words, he would get a new kidney and would not need to take the typical anti-rejection medications. Even though I had a perfect match with my sister (4 out of 4 versus a 2 out of 4, for a parent) I was told, he was better than perfect. It was as though they were putting his own kidney back into him. As he left the room that morning for the surgery, he wished me luck and hoped to see me in the isolation recovery section after our surgeries. To my surprise, he returned a couple of hours later after it was discovered during his twin brother's surgery, that his twin brother's selected kidney had cancer. If the doctors had selected the other kidney, his brother would have never known and would have possibly lost both of his kidneys and possibly worse died from the cancer. In a sense, the need for his twin brother's kidney had saved his brother's life. But it left my roommate without that "perfect match" kidney.

My surgery was successful, and while recovering in a private room, I began to realize I was regaining all my energy. I was not going to take this new opportunity for granted. As I had recently learned from my former roommates, we are thrown many obstacles in life and none of us know how much time we have or the type of road we will need to travel on. I now felt it was time; I was now ready to refocus my energy and start my preparation toward elder care. With all my energy and passion back, I began filling out applications in my hospital room for graduate school. I was now ready to embark on the additional training I needed. I needed to prove to myself that I could endure the stresses of graduate school. I needed to know I could feel normal again.

My acceptance to the MBA program at Babson College in Wellesley, Massachusetts, in fall of 1987, would turn out to have a direct correlation in everything I have done since with elder care. Babson College was well known for its entrepreneurial studies and MBA curriculum. As much as I needed business training, I also wanted to begin my elder studies too. I was fortunate that Babson professors allowed me to tie all my classes to some aspect of elder care. If there were research papers for the marketing class for example, my assignment would be marketing to elders. Every aspect of my business studies, business plans, and research touched some form of elder care. This strategic decision would lead to a string of meaningful connections that would become yet another turning point in my life.

Because of my pursuit to better understand elder care, however, I felt a little out of place on campus. This misplacement led to an awareness of my interests and goals by others. Because of this awareness, a strange, but meaningful coincidence would occur. Sherm White was a fellow student I would see in some classes and occasionally I would run into him in the café; once or twice we would share a meal together. It is fair to say that we were kind to each other, but we had separate lives outside of school. Somehow, I must have shared my interest in elder care with him during one of the brief lunches and he remembered.

One-day Sherm was making a phone call to someone in Wellesley and he mistakenly dialed the wrong number. Most, if not all of us, would apologize to the person on the other line and move onto the phone call that we needed to make. This was not the case for Sherm that day as he told me a couple of weeks later when he found me on campus. He told me he was in a strange mood and decided to speak to the stranger on the other end. The person on the other end had written books on elder care and was in fact an elder-care consultant. Sherm immediately told him about this guy at Babson interested in elder care too. Surprisingly, the gentleman gave Sherm his telephone number and asked him to pass it along to me.

Sherm found me on campus two weeks later and for some reason he was still carrying the telephone number. Of course, my curiosity was piqued and I called the gentleman, Bob Chellis, that evening. I set up a follow-up meeting; it was the beginning of a mentoring role he would play when I was ready to embark on a career in elder care. (Twenty-five years later I tracked Sherm down in Los Angeles to tell him about the impact of this event. At first, he did not remember who I was, but he eventually remembered the strange telephone call.)

During my studies at Babson, it became increasingly apparent to me that Scandinavia was many years ahead of the United States in programs for older adults. Coincidentally, after my graduation, Bob introduced me to an administrator who was retiring from running the Swedish Retirement Home in Newton, Massachusetts. This was a small facility overseen by the Swedish Charitable Society of Greater Boston. I was hired by Swedish Charitable Society in May of 1990, to work at the retirement home even though I was an outsider, not Scandinavian and still largely unfamiliar with Scandinavian culture. At first, I did not fully appreciate the implications of the Scandinavian caring philosophy, yet I felt that there was something right about their system. With time and personal experience, I have come to realize that Scandinavian ideas, beliefs and approaches to elder care are commonsense and natural.

Bob paid me a friendly visit to see how I was doing at the Swedish Home. After taking a tour of the Scandinavian Library, which was housed on the site of the Swedish Home, Bob suggested I take a research trip to Scandinavia. Through his assistance, I was fortunate to receive a grant from the

Charles Farnsworth Trust, and with the help of the Swedish Charitable Society of Greater Boston, I made two trips to Scandinavia — in 1993 and 1995 — visiting Denmark, Finland, Norway and Sweden to study their elder care principles. I was invited to visit over 60 facilities and meet with dozens of professionals in the senior-housing industry.

My trips to Scandinavia would lead me to rediscover the feelings that first drew me to working with elders. After returning to the United States, I began to realize the huge differences between the approaches to elder care in Scandinavia and the United States. This growing realization awakened an anger that stemmed from the experience I had as a young teenager. I now realized why the second hospitalization turned out to be a vastly different experience for me. Despite the seriousness of my situation, I remember this experience in a much more positive light. My three-week recuperation had required isolation from the public because of the danger of infection. The isolation wing consisted of all private rooms with bathrooms, yet I never felt isolated. I had control of my room, my space, my territory. When I wanted to socialize, I could. When I wanted to be alone, I could. Medical isolation was not a depressing or sad experience; it served to energize me and hastened my recuperation.

Other events fueled my anger. When I returned from my first trip to Scandinavia, I was told that in only three and a half weeks, six of the residents from the Swedish Retirement Home had been transferred to skilled nursing homes for short-term rehabilitation or permanent placement. These residents left their private rooms for rooms with two, three, or four beds. Before my trip, I would have found this to be acceptable and unremarkable, but now I had returned with a new awareness.

During a visit with a resident who had been transferred, she asked for help to go to the bathroom. There was so much concern about protocol and confusion about the staff's responsibility that her simple, but critical, request went unheeded until the activity director stepped forward and volunteered. Regrettably, the resident died that evening essentially alone and helpless. Later, I would discover that the activity director was reprimanded for her actions. In another nursing home, I was appalled to find one of the residents had been left undressed in bed in a four-bed, open room where one of her roommates was dying. She begged me to get her out of there. Fortunately, I was able to have her transferred back to the Swedish Retirement Home.

Four other residents passed away during this period under similar depressing circumstances in nursing homes. Sensing my uneasiness, a board member tried to console me by saying, "Try not to be upset over the deaths of these residents." What she did not realize was that I was not upset about their deaths, because I accept death as a natural part of life, but about the manner of their deaths. What I could not accept is the way our residents — or any other elders — are forced to live in an undignified, depressing, and, at times, uncivilized manner in institutional settings, especially at the end of their lives.

After explaining to an industry colleague about the "private rooms for all" concept found in all elder-care facilities in Denmark (and to a lesser extent in the other Scandinavian countries), her immediate reply to me was, "It's not practical here in the United States." It was at this point that I realized I had to demonstrate that the Scandinavian approach to senior housing in which they try to de-institutionalize the living environment for older adults while trying to maintain a natural connection to the surrounding community, was indeed practical in the United States and that my observations were strongly supported by American research.

Thus, in spring of 1995, I published *Unlimited Options for Aging*, which grew out of a young man's anger and determination to share exciting and innovative ideas with the widest possible American audience. In 2001, I helped to put my theories into action with the opening of the Scandinavian Living Center. Sixteen years later, my understanding of elder care has only deepened.

With this new book, I want to explore how we can transform our concepts and practice of housing and elder care. We must examine core beliefs of what it means to grow older and consider how these beliefs can influence the long-term care of the elder population. I am driven by the possibilities of developing the type of community in which natural connections can lead to positive outcomes for all. To evaluate, re-evaluate and re-direct attitudes and practices is to re-affirm the very essence of a growing, changing, aging population with the power to choose and to mold their personal and shared reality.

In our lifelong journeys, we encounter people of all ages. Some encounters are more meaningful than others, but they are natural connections that form life's opportunities and setbacks. Moments that help shape not only our personhood, but that of the people around us. These moments make you strong, keep you focused and influence your next steps. And along the way, you find yourself contributing to others.

In the pages that follow I will explain how I believe we can all contribute to better and more human care for our elder population.

CHAPTER 2

Challenges and the Power of Human Connections

Every one of us receives and passes on an inheritance.
The inheritance may not be an accumulation of earthly
possessions or acquired riches, but whether we realize
it or not, our choices, words, actions, and values will
impact someone and form the heritage we hand down.

Ben Hardesty

There are two ways of meeting old age. One is to resign to it, letting it take over your life; the other is to adjust to it, keeping in the stream of life and prodding oneself gently into the activities one can still do (Gross, 1978).[4]

I am reminded of two people whose differing experiences illustrate this. Their beliefs about retirement clearly influenced their approach to life. The first was a farmer who felt he had earned his time to sit back and relax. To him retirement meant literally sitting in his favorite chair and watching television every day. The people around him, including his family, also accepted this notion. So, sit he did, until he died two years later. The second person had worked in an office before her retirement. After retirement, she spent years volunteering at a retirement home and acting as financial secretary for the board of directors, until she eventually moved in as a resident at the age of 88. Living at the retirement home, she continued to make the bank deposits and read monthly reports to the board of directors, and each year she was nominated to continue as financial secretary. She often reminded me that "it was important to stay active and use your mind always."

When I first articulated the three priniciples for unlimited options for aging, I was focused on the individual elders who I had met and were now serving at the Scandinavian Living Center. I have come to realize that community-centered living forces us to look at these original principles and not by focusing just on the individual elder, but incorporating the entire community. This gives us a better opportunity to change the thinking about housing for all ages. For example:

- The principle of creating a positive residential reality was directed toward removing all aspects of an institutional setting for the individual elder. In the new book, this residential reality focuses more about authentic living, geared to creating a welcoming setting for all age groups to gather. Like our neighborhoods, authentic living involves all ages interacting. A residential reality leads to beautiful club-like settings, which is better than a hospital-like settings in most nursing homes or the old rest homes. But it is not authentic when the setting is not designed for the "entire" community.
- Encouraging our autonomy was meant to empower our elders to stay independent and take responsibility for their choices. Encouraging autonomy also means

creating a setting in which all ages are empowered to take responsibility in participating in a natural interaction with each other or the elders. In the past, I focused on the individual elder, but now I have come to realize that community-centered living forces us to encourage free choice for all ages and encourages residents to participate in a gathering environment created in a residential housing setting. It is a subtle difference, but it is important in understanding the concept that everything we do is based on the greater community and within that community, all ages are asked to take responsibility and to feel safe in a natural human interaction.

- Maintaining our lifestyle means focusing on the individual elder feeling comfortable in maintaining their hobbies and interests in a residential housing environment. However, what I have come to observe is that community-centered living goes beyond maintaining our hobbies or interests; it enables all of us, at any age, to maintain and recreate new hobbies or new interests. Maintaining our lifestyle becomes a byproduct of successful community-centered living.

It is important to emphasize that creating unlimited options for aging means accepting and encouraging as many choices as possible. In fact, some people choose to remain in their own homes, rather than move into elder housing. In many cases, the dwelling is then adapted to meet the evolving physical needs of the resident. Also, supportive home-care services are utilized to make this possible, based, not necessarily on age, but on the needs of the individual. These services might include regularly scheduled visits by a registered nurse. Thus, this is an option that should be part of consideration of lifestyle for an aging person.

Those who choose to move into a senior residence or assisted housing should not forgo the social benefits that come from staying in one's home, in a familiar neighborhood. The key to doing this stems from the important concept of connections — something that affected me personally and has helped me apply to my goals for community-centered living. Without human connections, we begin to lose our humanity. This was dramatically revealed to me in 1984.

————

During my 1984 trip to Haiti I stayed with the Missionaries of Charity Sisters, a group started by Mother Theresa. The buildings on the sisters' campus included a clinic for the nearby villages. This was where the villager came to get their food, find care for their family, and in some cases, abandon their babies in hopes for a better life for them. I do not remember the details of my work, but I remember an incident in which I found myself walking with a Sister through part of the orphanage filled with cribs. In some cases, there were two infants per crib. It was amazing to me that the babies seemed to be resting and were so quiet. Because of this, I naturally lowered my voice and started whispering to the worker. It was then that the worker turned to me and asked me why I was whispering. "I did not want to wake the babies," I whispered. No, she said, "They are not resting; they have stopped crying because no one is holding them or coming to them when they cry. Due to the staff shortage, we do not have enough nurses or volunteers to interact with the babies. The best we can do is give them a safe place to stay."

Because of the lack of human connection and lack of response to their cries for attention, the infants naturally turned inward and adjusted to their isolated world. Years later, I cannot stop feeling that this same impact is forced on individuals when they are separated from their community of human connections.

Decades later, as the Scandinavian Living Center was being completed in 2001, my son was getting ready to embark on his own life's journey. My boy, who had just turned five, was about to start kindergarten. How do you protect a little man when you cannot be there by his side? I concluded that I would give him a message, a tool, to help him interact with the unexpected. I decided to share a daily message, and I would make sure that when he was at the age that he stopped listening to me, my message would stay with him, consciously or unconsciously. So, each day, for 180 days a year, for 13 years (until he graduated from high school) before I dropped him off or before he left the house (over 2,300 times) he heard me say "Conquer your lows, capture your highs, be kind and find your funny bone." The poor kid, I gave new meaning to the phrase "You are repeating yourself."

The point I wanted to make is that he, like all of us, would have human connections that would seem terrible at times but at other times seem fantastic. My message to him was to conquer those low moments, not try to avoid them, but to accept the interaction and never fear your ability to overcome the labeling, the hurt, or the people trying to discourage you.

With the lows come those wonderful highs, those opportunities when angels fall from the sky in the form of strangers, neighbors, friends or family in which they share a moment of support, advice, encouragement or inspiration. Finally, I would add that he needed to laugh at life and the lows created by others. In a sense, the people creating obstacles or trying to discourage you are like the "silly fools" a king uses to create comic relief and distractions. Dr. Barbara Fredrickson refers to such daily efforts as "micro-moments," a connection with other people that can impact you socially, psychologically, and physically.[5]

It is this human connection that is an important ingredient for community-centered-living. I believe that the simple tool I shared with my son is a natural and important part of all human connections and a critical part of community-centered living. Understanding this and allowing all types of human interactions to happen is key to community-centered living, which is needed through the passage of life.

The impact of human connections can be both meaningless or life-changing as demonstrated in the following story. I was honored when my niece asked me to officiate her marriage. In doing so, I obtained a Justice of the Peace for a day and decided to incorporate the tools to deal with the passage-of-life message into the ceremony. During my speech, I discussed examples of angels (family and friends) that fall from the sky and step up and help you through difficult times. After the ceremony, I walked up to a relative in the audience to tell him that he was one of my examples. As I was pouring out my heart and thanking him, he stopped me and told me that he could not remember the incident and was not sure what I was talking about. I was stunned. How could he take such a powerful moment and reduce it to something meaningless to him?

I was becoming a little upset when, within a span of two minutes, I was interrupted in my thoughts by a friend of my niece. She said, "Joe, you were the reason I went to Harvard Business School to get my MBA." Suddenly, I had all these mixed emotions. What the heck was she talking about? In fact, initially, I did not recognize her. She went on to tell me that during a car ride, long forgotten and meaningless to me, I apparently said something that inspired her to pursue her MBA at Harvard. It was from that day forward, she said, a new goal was set. Within a course of three minutes, two impactful vs. meaningless human connections occurred. Such incidents have helped me realize that community-centered living encourages independence and interdependence grounded in interactions that can seem inconsequential to one participant while profoundly impacting the other.

A Chinese dance demonstration that I once attended illustrates this point. The dancers represented the five elements: metal, wood, water, fire and earth. Each was a separate and independent entity, but they were all intimately connected, each alternating in an endless cyclical and symbiotic way. The separation and intimacy of the elements made for a beautiful dance, but it also symbolized the human interactions that exist from cradle to grave. Trying to eliminate any part of this community interaction can lead to negative consequences.

A community of human connections develops within an ecosystem in which all ages interact. This is the mission of community-centered living — to focus on the larger population and to welcome everyone in that community. As we walk through life we are given the opportunity to visit with people, to visit the world, and to dream about goals. As we get older, the ability to visit, travel or dream can feel limited. It is this limitation, this potential low, that community-centered living addresses and tries to overcome.

Charles H. Vogl writes about a 75-year study of adult development in which "people who are socially disconnected are less happy, experience health declines earlier, and live shorter lives than people who are not lonely. One in five people report that they are lonely. In referring to all ages, he says, "The number of people who say that they have no one to talk to about difficult subjects has tripled in the last four decades."[6]

When creating housing communities for older adults, we must be aware of the need to connect this senior housing with the town or the surrounding neighborhood. If this connection is lost, which is the case in many elder housing communities, we have created an invisible wall that separates and isolates our elders from the surrounding neighborhood. It is this separation that leads to isolationist thinking on the part of the elders, a mentality that can lead elders within a housing community to refer to friends and neighbors as the "outside community." This separation can also lead to the "outside community" dismissing and devaluing these elders living inside these segregated communities.

The fact that we often locate senior housing in isolated or secluded settings away from ordinary community activities sends the wrong message that aging and retirement mean withdrawal from ordinary life. Thus, finding ways to bring neighbors and friends of all ages together is an important element of community-centered-living.

Community-centered living breaks down the walls of separation that leads to isolated living, but more importantly, it allows those who are limited physically or mentally to stay naturally connected to the surrounding world.

CHAPTER 3

A Welcoming Place for All: Creating A Positive Residential Reality

Regarding elder housing: Institutionalism produces a genuine neurosis that has the characteristics of loss of contact with the outside world, enforced idleness, bossiness of medical and nursing staff; loss of personal friends, possessions, and personal events — ward atmosphere and loss of prospects outside the institution.

(Bowker, 1982)[7]

My own wedding was a lesson in the importance of community-centered living.

To explain: I discovered Elizabeth Seton Residence in Wellesley, Massachusetts, during my research trips of model nursing homes in America and it quickly became first choice for my future mother-in-law when skilled care became necessary. To make sure she could attend the wedding, my fiancé and I decided to get married in the nursing home's lovely outdoor courtyard. What became apparent during the planning and performance of the wedding was that the residents and staff became very connected to the idea of "outside people" sharing an important part of their life. In a sense, we felt like a part of their community because residents and staff were able to witness our wedding from their setting.

For a long time after the wedding, residents, staff, and family members would stop us to remark about the wedding and how much they enjoyed it. I was amused initially, but quickly realized that the ceremony represented a type of human connection and reinforced in me the need to create an atmosphere for connecting residents to their neighbors, the "outside community." It was at this point I started realizing that having a positive welcoming residential setting meant there was responsibility to utilize this component to create human connection through the principle of community-centered living.

My initial understanding about a positive residential setting was limited to the need for creating more private rooms in nursing homes, and more homelike environments in assisted living and other forms of elder care housing. As important as private rooms became in the design of a welcoming residential setting, I now realize the important impact of having multiple common gathering spaces for people to gather.

As a nursing home, Elizabeth Seton Residence offers an outpatient physical therapy program for their residents and has been exploring the possibility of offering these programs to families and neighbors. In a small way the administration is beginning to realize the importance of ongoing community connection beyond the physical design of private rooms.

Elizabeth Seton Winter Garden

Elizabeth Seton Courtyard

If done right, people living in elder-care housing — ranging from nursing homes, assisted living to independent living settings — as well as the surrounding neighborhood can benefit. Creating and implementing a successful community-centered living program involves developing a housing complex that has a welcoming residential setting for everyone. It should be a physical structure that welcomes not only individuals living within the walls of the housing complex, but the entire surrounding neighborhood. To make this happen it is important to understand the components necessary to create a welcoming and positive residential setting.

This involves more than just the cosmetic look or appeal; there is also a need for community spaces at which people may gather. The "wow" factor during the first impression draws people in, but it is important to sustain community connection. To develop an atmosphere of community involvement that encourages multiple visits, the housing complex needs to become a central gathering place for organizations and people with common interest in the surrounding neighborhood.

In a sense, it needs to become the coffee shop or the old-fashion general store in which stories are shared and gathering crowds are encouraged. Thus, physical structure with enough different common spaces becomes an important component of a positive and welcoming residential reality.

When creating a welcoming residential setting for all, the goal needs to go beyond building a housing facility to house only individual people, but rather includes creating a place to welcome the surrounding community. The primary goal is to create an environment for all ages to gather. The housing project succeeds when visitors are unaware that the living arrangement is part of the housing complex.

An example of this occurred at an annual ice cream social that takes place at a traditional assisted living community, the Scandinavian Living Center. A mother once told me her children have no idea that they are coming to a traditional assisted living community. To them the Scandinavian Living Center is "a place to have ice cream and have fun."

Scandinavian facilities, as physical structures, generally blend into the community aesthetically, but often they serve other purposes that reflect the neighborhood's character and values. For example, in the village of Taarbæk, Denmark, the community moved a 130-year-old building 50 meters and remodeled it for use as a community center. At the same time 14 additional units for elder housing were added. The municipality leader told me it was not financially practical to make such a move, but the building had historical significance. Moreover, the facility is rented by civic and other organizations. Therefore, in a very tangible way, the community center and elder housing have become a central and vital part of the neighborhood.

In addition to creating welcoming common spaces, housing options for elders should be residential and homelike. Any form of institutional design can become a barrier for connecting with others. Denmark continues to lead the way in elder housing initiatives because the Danes emphasize the importance of maintaining a normal living arrangement for the resident with minimal institutionalization. The best housing units I saw utilize a universal design appropriate for all age groups and are equipped with adaptive devices to allow for the special needs of an aging resident.

For example, the stove only works if a timer is also turned on. The counter and cabinet height can be adjusted up or down to accommodate wheelchair-bound or very short residents. Bathrooms are equipped with roll-in showers which allow a resident to roll in a wheelchair. Sinks can be raised or lowered with the touch of a lever. Heated bathroom floors are comfortable and the heat helps dry up water, preventing mildew build-up and reducing accidental falls. A washer/dryer is becoming standard and is usually found in the bathroom. These adaptive appliances allow a person to function with minimal assistance or dependence on staff. A welcoming residential setting is when the opportunities or choices are not lost through design, but rather design helps eliminate and overcome the obstacles created in an institutional setting, giving us the ability to focus our energy on our individual needs and goals. Creating a positive residential setting that is both comfortable and safe will make it easier for individuals to reach out and connect with the broader community.

Think about how you choose an apartment to rent. You make a careful inspection of the unit, its configuration and the surrounding landscape and setting. You also weigh how the dwelling might satisfy your own personal preferences, interests and lifestyle. Would you choose to move into a complex where the management made all these choices, even to the point of assigning roommates?

Another way of looking at the existence of institutional reality is the impact on our thinking. This can occur when residents move into a beautiful housing complex. The complex may have the best design with wonderful amenities creating a homelike environment, but if the residents look out a window of the complex and refer to their neighbors as the "outside community" then institutional thinking continues to exist.

Our own institutional thinking can be an obstacle in choosing to join friends from the neighborhood or being part of a larger group. Institutional reality is the limiting of our current opportunities or choices because of the design and institutional beliefs of the public.

Why does this institutional thinking exist and what has caused these beliefs to be part of our everyday thinking that challenges us in creating a welcoming residential setting in all forms of elder housing? To understand the obstacles and outdated thinking, it is important to take a brief look at the history of elder care and what was put in place as a solution during the early part of the 20th century.

At the beginning of the 20th century as people began to live longer and family support for elders began to decline, we needed a solution to care for our aging population. The design of much senior housing in the United States then was developed from the acute-care hospital model. For years, elders lived in these hospital-like structures sharing rooms with strangers. These outdated hospital-like dwellings invited residents to be viewed as "patients." This label, "patient," in turn connotes a sense of sickness and dependence.[8] Creating elder care housing models based on hospital-like design and efficiency for short-term stays, instilled the idea that once you moved into this type of facility, it was more important to be safe and cared for than to stay connected to your neighbors and friends. It was this thinking and this belief experienced by many generations, that allowed us to look at old age as triggering an abrupt change from a familiar, natural, residential setting to an unfamiliar, highly structured and unnatural institutional setting.

Studies have shown that an environment that strips away one's control and erases any possible personal choice can have a definite, negative effect on the quality of one's life[9; 10]. Even the well-meaning unthinkingly consented to a controlling, numbing environment for our grandparents, our parents, and even ourselves.

It was this setting that instilled a sense of separation from elders, who were thought to need extra care. We did not feel comfortable nor did we want to socialize in a sterile setting. It was uncomfortable, but more importantly, it became more isolating for the people living in this type of hospital-like housing model.

To further add to the isolation, the hospital-like design utilizing shared rooms sometimes developed territorial boundaries for the residents, causing a withdrawal from multiple human connections[11; 12; 13]. This was illustrated in a story a woman told me about her aunt. "My aunt becomes very angry when her roommate places anything on her side of the room. Simply crossing this imaginary line often leads to heated debates." Most of this woman's time was spent making sure no one stepped into her space. Further studies confirm that residents in shared units viewed their dwelling as less secure and they felt less able to control social encounters occurring there.[14]

This institutional reality was the reason my original trips to Scandinavia had a powerful impact on how I looked at our entire elder-care industry. The residential and physical design of Elizabeth Seton Residence come close to emulating what I witnessed in Scandinavia. Coincidentally, this nursing home was also inspired by a trip to Scandinavia. Administrator Laurie Ferrante says, "The Sisters were ahead of their time in constructing private rooms clustered in modules, or neighborhoods. The same Small House design is now the trend as skilled nursing facilities renovate to create private resident rooms grouped in small homelike units. The design is not only appropriate for long-term care, but also successful for fostering a comfortable and therapeutic milieu in post-acute rehabilitation units."

One part of maintaining a welcoming residential setting means establishing natural housing configurations in neighborhoods with mixed populations. In Scandinavian housing projects, age groups are mixed as in any other neighborhood but they live in different clustering arrangements. The Danish view is that isolating a certain group of people (in this case the elders) and providing a separate physical setting for them is a step toward institutionalism. By building facilities with a universal design for all age groups, segregation and isolation will not occur. In a welcoming residential reality, different age groups can continue to coexist with dignity and mutual respect.

I found an example of a creative project with a mixed-population of residents in Malmö, Sweden. In this complex, a group of seniors were housed in cluster-style apartment units. Residents had their own private rooms each with full bathroom, and shared a kitchen, dining room and living room with the group. In this senior section, there was usually one staff person present 24 hours a day. In other clusters, one found young singles or couples with children.

Years later, I would be reminded of this design with the development of the Leonard Florence Center for Living in Chelsea, Massachusetts, a project influenced by Dr. Bill Thomas, and developed and brought to fruition by Barry Berman. (See Chapter 7.)

Certainly, elder housing should ensure its residents do not feel isolated. But there's another factor just as important: Autonomy.

CHAPTER 4

Embracing Autonomy

*America was founded on independence — the freedom
to approach life, including one's morals, attitude, and
preferred entertainment and fashions—in a manner
appropriate to one's individuality.*

(Webster's Dictionary)

n the context of elder care, independence is the freedom
from external control or unwanted influence in one's residential setting.

A professional colleague once questioned my private
room requirement as it applies to older adults living in nursing homes. He believed that shared rooms can facilitate social
interaction.

My response was that private versus shared isn't the issue.
The issue is autonomy; a person must have the freedom
to choose whether to be in a shared unit or a private unit.
Institutional reality dominates when choice is eliminated.

The freedom to choose between a private or a shared room enables an older adult to live in a residential setting that is right for him or her. More importantly, by supporting an elder's right to choose, society demonstrates its regard for that senior. This is the right to autonomy. Embracing autonomy as well as creating a welcoming residential setting is important for promoting natural social interaction and successful community-centered living.

If you value your right to make choices, but do not acknowledge your responsibility to insure other people's right to make choices for themselves, it implies that you do not value the other person. Restricting autonomy promotes constricted "institutional" thinking, unhealthy human connections, and resistance to exploring healthy options.

As the story goes, Moses came down from the mountain with two tablets filled with the Ten Commandments. Centuries later, to simplify and consolidate the messages in the commandments, Jesus proposed the Golden Rule. This was a simple and powerful message that instructed us to treat people the way we would like other people to treat us. It's a powerful concept — and very challenging to put into practice.

This is the problem with autonomy as well. It can be challenging to support. Yet implicit in the framework of the Ten Commandments and the Golden Rule is our God-given right to choose — our autonomy. Good or bad, autonomy and our freedom to choose, directs every decision and action we make. When we try to disregard this right, we create a recipe for disaster.

When we put ourselves in the position to limit other people's decision-making opportunities, we limit the possibilities for healthy social interactions. As long as one's decision does not harm others, we need to continue to encourage personal decision-making. If not, limiting a person's ability to choose can lead to painful consequences.

Take the mischievous story of a 96-year-old man and his path to autonomous living. This gentleman had been extremely successful in his lifetime even though he only had a fourth-grade education. He was a self-educated person who helped raise six children with his wife of 70 years. His children were reared knowing the value of hard work and the importance of a good education; they went on to get undergraduate, graduate and medical degrees to become successful professionals.

In his later years, the man tried to encourage his wife to move to supportive housing with him, but she refused saying, she wanted to die in her home. However, as time passed, the wife increasingly needed medical care and was eventually separated (by her children) from her husband, ultimately ending up in an assisted living community. At this point, however, the husband now refused to leave his house. His children, with doctors, nurses, protective services, law enforcement, social workers and lawyers, all thought they knew better. But they forgot the power of individual control. The man's will to control his autonomy was stronger than his lack of ability.

The 96-year-old father — a "helpless Italian husband" — taught himself to cook, do laundry, and keep the house clean. For seven months, from September to April, he took control of his life and refused to take the advice from his children and the professionals around him. This man, from the great generation who fought in World War II, survived and became even stronger. He was determined to control his life. His children, however, suffered unhealthy stress from worry trying to understand their father's decision.

During this time, the father visited other assisted living communities and investigated alternatives for his wife and him. The final decision, he insisted, would be "theirs alone." Unknown to the children, the father was also having discussions with residents and staff of the assisted living community where his wife lived. Quietly and slowly, he began to move his clothes into her apartment. The children and the professionals were unaware of his actions until he told them he would move in with his wife for a two-month trial on — not coincidentally, April Fool's Day. In this symbolic gesture, he demonstrated his control and reminded all his children that we are foolish when we try to take a person's autonomy away.

The senior housing industry should reaffirm and reinforce the right of adults to assume responsibility for themselves. Self-responsibility should not end at 60, 70, 80 or even older. This may have unexpected benefits as shown by the following experiment: A nursing-home study compared two similar groups (matched for age, health, and sex) from different floors within the same facility. One group consisted of residents who were told they were responsible for caring for themselves. The other group consisted of residents who were encouraged to feel that the staff would care for them and try to make them happy. There was in fact little or no difference in the amount of attention paid to the two groups; however, there were major differences in the language used by the administrator and his staff, as outlined here:

Encouraged Responsibility for Self	Encouraged to Have Staff Care
• **You** are responsible for your care.	• **We** will help care for you.
• **You** decide whether you want to make this a home.	• **We** will help you make this a home.
• **You** decide how you want to have your room set up.	• **We** have set up your room.
• If **you** are unsatisfied you have influence to change it.	• **We** will see if we can make some changes.
• Movies are Tuesday and Thursday; let us know which night **you** want to go.	• **We** will schedule the movie night for you.
• Choose a plant as a gift; **you** must water it.	• **We** are handing our plants to all of you; the nurse will water it for you.

The study concluded that the responsibility-induced group was more active and reported they felt happier. This same group showed a significant improvement in alertness and behavioral involvement in activities. Ninety-three percent of the responsibility group showed overall improvement, whereas seventy-one percent of the dependency-induced group became more debilitated.[15]

An illustration of taking individual responsibility occurred at the Scandinavian Living Center, which was designed with single-loaded corridors (windows on one side of the corridor and apartments on the other side) that encircle an outdoor courtyard. There was an unexpected benefit to this design when Edna moved to the SLC at the age of 90 and began to use the single-loaded corridor for daily walks. She preferred to forego our leading-edge fitness equipment and walk around this "indoor track." And walk she did! A retired bookkeeper, Edna enjoyed taking careful numeric notes and tracked her miles each day (thirteen times around made a mile). Edna had walked over 3,000 miles before she left us at age 100. The welcoming residential design made this possible; the choice was hers, and she demonstrated how she wanted to define her quality of life.

Another important way of promoting and maintaining autonomy is the use of appropriate technology and assistive devices. Effective technology can compensate for a person's physical impairment, improving quality of life, and in some cases, decrease or eliminate the need for institutional placement. Without appropriate devices, (for example, the technology used to help the person with ALS discussed in Chapter 7) many aging individuals would need someone to assist them in simple tasks. When people are encouraged to be more independent through technology, they become more comfortable making choices such as going to a basketball game and looking forward to going to a baseball game. Belief, practice, and technology make us more self-reliant and less dependent on decisions made by others. When people are allowed to live in a welcoming residential setting with the use of technology when needed, it becomes easier for them to feel empowered to take responsibility for their lives and actions.

Using technology and design, one can promote some degree of autonomy even in people with severe cognitive impairment. In a small housing facility near Sandefjord, Norway, ten residents with dementia lived in private rooms with full bathrooms, but shared a common dining room, living room, and kitchen. They were cared for by one person from 7 a.m. to midnight. However, between midnight and 7 a.m. the residents were alone. There were passive alarms connected to doors and walkways. If a person wandered out of his or her private room, a silent alarm would notify staff in another facility nearby. Surprisingly, in one year only two wandering incidents occurred in this facility.

Americans have come a long way in embracing the importance of autonomy. It has become part of our common-sense thinking. In some cases, as we age our physical and mental capacity diminishes. It is extremely important that society and the people involved as caregivers understand the significance of providing different alternatives for choice. Even when our abilities are limited, it remains important that we still have control over some basic decisions. Simply stated, when we support self-determination, a person's ability to choose, we value them and encourage them to stay connected to the world around them.

Encouraging responsibility through autonomy occurs when several forces work together. For a person to feel he can make his own decisions he must be supported by a culture that fosters and promotes autonomy through a variety of opportunities and choices. Respect for each person's needs and expectations is achieved through open-mindedness, physical design, and technology. One must aim at continuity in life, so that the passage to old age is not experienced as a radical rupture from the previous lifestyle, but a welcoming opportunity to continue to participate in the world by maintaining their chosen lifestyle.

CHAPTER 5

Maintaining One's Lifestyle

*Whatever we possess becomes of double value when we
have the opportunity of sharing it with others.*

Jean-Nicolas Bouilly

We confirm our reality by sharing.

Barbara Grizzuti Harrison

No one understood the importance of maintaining a
lifestyle through all stages of life better than my friend,
Al Henick. I met Al when I was running the Swedish
Home. He was familiar with my research trips to Scandinavia
and the principles developed from my research. During this
time, Al started a small appliance repair group for another
local nonprofit, and the group met weekly at the Swedish
Home, and later at the new Scandinavian Living Center. This

wonderful group repairs small appliances for neighbors in the community and only charges for parts. All of us have brought small appliances to them over the years and have benefited from their talent.

Al, a retired engineer, was an intelligent man interested in many subjects. Al would sit with me and discuss my research and the development of the four principles. He watched with amazement, as we developed the Scandinavian Living Center (SLC) utilizing the principles from the research. Over time, during our weekly contacts and many discussions, we became comfortable with each other. This led to a special friendship and friendly bantering. Sadly, after the Scandinavian Living Center was built, Al's wife passed away. Eventually Al decided that he wanted to move into the SLC.

I was thrilled by this decision and could not stop myself from asking why he chose the SLC. I was sure he would tell me it was because of our friendship... perhaps he would tell me that it was because I was a great guy. At the very least I was confident that he would tell me that it was because of the research, the principles behind the design and philosophy. Instead, without any hesitation, he told me that he decided to move into the SLC because his toolbox was there and "I do not feel like moving it."

Through his tongue-in-cheek humor, (and may I add his quick wit and intelligence), he was telling me he was moving to the SLC because we were giving him the best opportunity to maintain his lifestyle, his connection to the community, and his friends. Without spelling it out for me, he was complimenting me. Al, if you are listening, I have always been honored by the fact that you moved to the SLC because your toolbox was there.

Before older adults can take responsibility for themselves, they need to feel comfortable with their surrounding environment. Most importantly, they must feel they can express themselves within the context of their own lifestyle; that was the case with Al.

A fundamental difference between life in Scandinavia and in the United States is that in Scandinavia the integrity and continuity of life is maintained as one passes through different stages. In Denmark, old age is thought of as a continuation of life that is based on one's own resources and wishes and dominated by needs and interests just as in youthful years.[16] For each person to maintain his or her lifestyle, with dignity, we must accept aging as a natural and healthy process. In some cases, we must allow those with physical challenges to express themselves differently or as needed.

A speaker at a recent fundraiser for Sounds of Recovery, a nonprofit organization that specializes in music therapy, discussed how health-care personnel tend to focus on fixing a patient's problem rather than focusing on other existing talents and inspirations that could positively impact their care. By bringing ages together and creating opportunities for people to share their talents, community-centered living creates possibilities for inspiration. This inspiration can lead to healthier lifestyles.

During my research trips to Scandinavia, in the 1990s, I made many mistakes while questioning the Scandinavians about their system of elder care. I often showed the bias of my American vocabulary and perspective in these discussions. For example, I would ask about the number of beds in a facility instead of asking for the number of rooms. When I asked Paul Holbek, an administrator of a nursing home and assisted living community, how the "very sick" elderly are cared for, he was surprised by my comment. His reply was simple and direct: "Residents are not sicker in nursing homes — just frail; it is normal to be incontinent or senile. You are still living; it is normal for you to be old. It is a normal process to get old and decrease in function—but you are still living." Every effort, he said, should be made to encourage the aging person to continue living, not to encourage dying.

Others echoed his comments. Lisbeth Sorensen, a Danish nursing home administrator, said, "People who are handicapped and 65-plus are looked at as sick. They are not sick, but healthy with unique disabilities." Hans Rasmussen, a Danish researcher, told me: "Even becoming ill does not mean you are a sick person; developing illness is a normal part of life." During an interview at the University of Stockholm, Dr. Mats Thorslund told me, "It is normal to become incontinent or unable to walk, etc. . . . It is part of life . . . Home help, emergency response systems, lifts on buses, and technology in general allow a person to stay independent with dignity. You do not have to stereotype them or label them as sickly."

As summarized by Arne Nielsen, a Danish industry executive, we need to ask our elders: "Who are you, what can you do for yourself, what have you done in the past and what are your interests?"

Negative labeling of older adults can lead to deterioration in performance despite any previously experienced success. Simply calling people "elderly" with all the pejorative implications that go with it encourages seniors to be more passive. With negative labeling, whether explicit or implied, we are suggesting that they are less capable of living independently or maintaining their previous lifestyle.[17]

There is ample evidence that labels can influence attitudes and behavior. For example, a study of people working together demonstrated that individuals given low-status labels, such as "assistant" drew unnecessary influence from and became more dependent on the person who was labeled boss; they became less able to perform tasks they were able to perform successfully before they were given the label "assistant".[18]

The study above reminds me of an incident in Haiti while I was studying how an impoverished nation cares for its elders. As stated earlier, I stayed with a group run by Mother Theresa's organization whose mission was to teach Haitians to become more self-sufficient. Instead of just feeding the hungry, they would be paid for work "in kind" with food and water, thus maintaining their self-respect and dignity. While we were unloading a truck, I was responsible for telling the workers, who were very quiet and passive, where to place bags of food. At one point, I asked one of the men to come into the truck to assume my role while I assisted the others in bringing the bags into the storage building. The person in the truck became noticeably more vocal and more active. Recognizing this, I decided to ask each of the men in turn to take charge. The response was always the same: they all began to ask if they could be in charge. Even though I had not labeled anyone the boss, the effect was obvious and immediate. Even giving them more implied responsibility measurably increased their self-esteem and productivity.

Negative labeling can clearly affect the experiences of older adults. Labels also shape the actual perception of staff toward their clients. This was convincingly demonstrated in an experiment done at Yale University where experienced therapists were shown a videotape of a man during an interview in which he discussed his recent job experiences. They were then asked to evaluate him with several measures. Prior to viewing the tape, half the therapists were told the interviewee was a "patient" and half were told he was a "job applicant." The therapists who saw the video after being told the interviewee was a patient stated that they believed his behavior was pathological.

On the other hand, the therapists who were told that he was an applicant thought his behavior was well-adjusted.[19]

Older adults are very vulnerable to becoming passive because "they bear negative labels. If they do not engage in previous responsibilities or activities, it is because we tend to do everything for them. We feel they have earned this moment to sit back and let us wait on them. However, this increased dependence leads to a loss of one's perceived control and eventually the fall of self-esteem."[20, 21]

In the 1960s a Swedish physiologist experimented with two groups of healthy young adults who were active and physically fit. He put both groups in bed for three weeks. One group was not allowed to get out of bed at all; they received total assistance in their activities of daily living. The other group was allowed to stand for just five minutes every day. After three weeks, all the participants had their physical aerobic ability measured. It was found that the bedridden group lost over twenty years of physical ability. By comparison, the other group who stood for only five minutes a day lost little of their ability.[22] These findings support the idea that maintaining an active lifestyle can help promote wellness and slow the aging process. They also illustrate the negative effects of enforced inactivity.

According to project leader Astrid Toft of the Sund Community in Norway, the best way to maintain residents' self-respect is not to help or take over, but to encourage the client to use his own resources as long as possible. Studies have shown that there is greater satisfaction for seniors when they are participating in a constructive way such as fundraising, bookkeeping, baby-sitting etc.[23] Individuals must believe they can maintain and be responsible for their own lifestyle. By restricting them, we condemn them to a setting which is predetermined, structured and institutionalized.

Henning Kirk, M.D., of the Danish Gerontological Institute asserts, "Defining service according to type of dwelling leads to regimentation of attitudes and roles, destroying the individuality of the old person. Instead, service should be provided according to the needs of the individual elder, independent of the person's housing."[24] The answer is not what others think is better for older people; it is what each individual thinks is appropriate for him/herself.

Studies have shown that people tend to maintain their same life patterns and preferences as they age. For instance, if they entertained friends at home and ate in restaurants when young, they will — and should —maintain the same pattern into old age. "Lifestyles including our attitudes and expectations may have more of an effect than age in predicting the quality of our lives."[25]

"In a homelike atmosphere . . . it is easier to fulfill basic needs for continuity and close contact with the family and to preserve personal integrity; these are needs which are difficult to meet in an institutional setting."[26] Therefore, striving for the best design for retirement housing or nursing homes should mean striving for a high quality of life and independence in a homelike, friendly atmosphere. Quality of life, as explained by Ann-Catherine Mattiasson and Lars Anderson, "should include, among other things, the right to be offered conditions governing one's life which are in accordance with one's own values."[27]

CHAPTER 6

Community-Centered Living in Action

P eople use the expression "it takes a village." I say it takes a healthy and vibrant neighborhood. Without a serious commitment to community-centered living and negation of the outdated belief that the removal and isolation of elders is normal, then the opportunity for natural, healthy and vibrant connections can be lost to all. Simply stated, there is no village.

Developing and designing the Scandinavian Living Center, a traditional assisted living community, was exciting. At the time, we focused on the principles from Unlimited Options for Aging, but we understood the importance of creating community-centered living with its vital links among all generations. We were guided by three important considerations.

First, the SLC had to become an inviting gathering place that promoted social interaction between residents and neighbors from the community at large. Second, residents of the SLC needed encouragement to engage more actively in the programs and services of the Center and thereby experience a greater connection to their neighbors and friends. Finally, we knew that as we created a community center mentality with its associated programs within an elder housing residence, our efforts would be under continuous public scrutiny.

The development of community-centered housing at the SLC began with the physical design of the building. Unlike most stand-alone assisted living communities, 50 percent of our building is dedicated to common area spaces. These common areas include a stunning performance venue (the Nordic Hall), a state-of-the-art fitness center, office space, the Scandinavian Library and the Kaffestugan café, all open to the public on specific days and times. Taking a page from the Forsmannsenteret experience, (see Chapter 7) we invited all the Scandinavian clubs as well as several organizations in the community to make the Center their home base. Our goal was to create the opportunity for SLC residents to participate in social groups that include the wider community.

As sound as our plan seemed, we learned an important lesson. Social interaction cannot be forced; it must occur naturally. In the early phase of the project, we spoke with the Newton Recreation Department and learned that the Department needed our Nordic Hall as a venue for its local card-playing group. We hoped that SLC residents would join the card players and interact with their new neighbors. To our surprise, the SLC residents resisted because they considered the card players to be "the outside community." It became eminently clear that an extremely well-designed building did not automatically break down the invisible institutional wall; a wall created by the residents' assimilation of our culture's inside-the-institution versus outside-the-institution perspective. We still needed to find a way to create natural connections to the "outside community."

We began by encouraging the residents to play cards in a separate part of the building on the same day as the Recreation Department card group. The resident card players then moved into the Nordic Hall where they played at tables alongside those of the Recreation Department card players. Eventually, some residents joined the Recreation Department card group. And then, some of the Recreation Department card players decided to move into the SLC as residents, making the community interconnection real.

Renting office space to a physical therapy company also taught us not to force community interaction but let it evolve naturally. An early anecdote involved a teenage boy who came to the SLC for physical therapy accompanied by his mother. At first, both son and mother questioned whether an assisted living community was the right therapeutic environment for a teenager. Within a week, the question was moot. The teenager had begun to drop by the café to share drinks and conversation with the residents. As I witnessed this new bond, I marveled at its sharp contrast to the negative experience I had as a teenager. My observation of this warm interaction between a young person and much older adults was another step in my increased understanding of the impact and importance of natural connections facilitated by the community-centered living principle. "Institutional walls," created by societal misperception and prejudices, can evaporate and disappear through natural and healthy connections.

Renting office space to Newton at Home (NAH), a nonprofit organization like the SLC, was a further step in the development of our community-centered housing model. NAH uses members and volunteers to help keep seniors in their homes and out of "retirement housing." When asked why we wanted to help this group, our answer was simple. To sustain unlimited options for aging, there must be many choices; we should not try to limit our choices to models such as older adult housing communities, continuing care retirement communities, assisted living, or other types of retirement housing.

As had happened in previous connections with the wider community, interaction between NAH members and our residents took place in unexpected ways. For example, Cleo, a 102-year-old SLC resident, began volunteering for NAH. Cleo took on the job of calling an 87-year-old home-bound gentleman to check on his well-being. It was fascinating to observe a resident of an assisted living community checking on the safety of a neighbor living at home in the surrounding community — a small example of a natural and healthy connection. It did not matter where Cleo lived. It was important that she created a connection.

From the beginning, sharing our principles and bringing visitors to the Scandinavian Living Center were very important to me. However, I wanted the public's understanding of the principles, especially the principle of community connection, to happen in a natural way — not through lectures, but through examples. I wanted the community to understand the thrill of connecting to others through a variety of opportunities. Instead of using typical marketing strategies to bring in referrals, such as hosting blood pressure clinics and offering lectures about financial planning and the difficulties of old age, I wanted our staff to be creative. I would always say, "Let the other facilities reinforce and remind people of being old and unhealthy. I do not want us to focus on the end of life. Everyone understands they are getting older. I would go on to say, "I prefer to have a yo-yo show...." This became the standard line when we discussed marketing outreach. And to my amusement and surprise, our marketing director decided to schedule an actual yo-yo show. We publicized free yo-yos as a treat for all the children. Amazingly, we sold out and had to turn people away.

We were delighted to learn at the show that an older member of the audience was a former Duncan Yo-Yo Champion. Sometime during the show, he began to demonstrate his yo-yo skills in front of the awestruck children and their parents. Another surprise occurred when a 93-year-old resident of the Living Center introduced a handcrafted yo-yo that he had made when he was eight years old. We quickly discovered that this 85-year-old wooden yo-yo worked much better than the yo-yos we passed out to the children. These older adults were not "boring" or "in the way" — they were exciting!

And there it was, older adults influencing a younger generation. In this brief and fun-filled connection "old-timers" were transformed into "elders of importance who had something valuable to share."

There is a perception that young adults and their children do not want to be surrounded by elders who have physical limitations. Even the "young old" (the healthy and active 65-75 population) say they do not want to be around "sick" older people. It has been shown that this avoidance stems from not knowing how to respond or act with people who are different. Increasing a person's exposure and allowing the opportunity to interact with those who are physically impaired can lead to better understanding (Langer, 1989 [48]). Familiarity eventually leads to adjustments, and those of differing abilities can socialize comfortably. We ran into the same push-back in the development of the Scandinavian Cultural Center, housed inside the SLC. People would ask, "Why would someone want to come to an assisted living facility to be part of a performance or a program?" Some would go on to say, "I would feel awkward or uncomfortable seeing elders with walkers/wheelchairs." As in any type of positive exposure, these concerns became non-issues once the real interactions occurred. Today, it is natural; all generations will reach out to each other in a more natural and humane way.

———

The establishment of the Scandinavian Cultural Center accomplished two important things. First, it honored the Scandinavian cultures that provided the inspiration for our model. Secondly, it created opportunities for our whole community, both within and beyond the Center, to come together. The residents of the SLC can walk down the hall and enjoy a world-class pianist free of charge. Their friends and family members can join them for concerts, art gallery receptions, Nordic film screenings and speakers. In addition, an annual Nordic food festival welcomes hundreds of people to the Center. Visitors are often surprised to find that the Cultural Center is located inside an assisted living community. But the homey and inviting atmosphere, the gorgeous Scandinavian architecture, colors and décor, and the Nordic programming that is unique in the region quickly draws them in. As a business model, incorporating the Cultural Center into the same space as the Living Center is beneficial to both partners. The partnership enables the Cultural Center to flourish because it receives operating support typically unavailable to small non-profits. The residents of the SLC benefit because they are given more opportunities to connect with the community-at-large during Cultural Center events.

The connection to the surrounding community became apparent when we were raising the funds needed to purchase a new Steinway B grand piano valued at close to $100,000. Within a short few months, we not only raised the necessary money, but also, on the last night of our final push, a member of the wider community literally threw money at us as we were speaking. There seemed to be a clear understanding that we were simultaneously raising money for a new piano and raising awareness of our community-centered living model.

The impact of community-centered living goes beyond connecting different generations. Offering an environment that encourages people to come together creates an opportunity to reconnect with old friends. During a Cultural Center performance, two neighbors who had not been together in over twenty years ran into each other. Their chance to connect, reminisce and plan a future get-together was a direct result of the opportunity created by our community-centered living model.

In the past, residents' family members became active participants of the Scandinavian Living Center community, and many warm relationships developed. Sadly, when residents moved out or passed away, those family relationships ended abruptly. There was no compelling reason for the families and friends of residents to remain connected to the Center. Now, by way of the many programs offered at the Cultural Center, we are discovering that families of former residents are returning to the Center and we are staying connected.

Potential family members now visit the Center before there is any need to research assisted living residences on a loved one's behalf. The families and friends of residents sometimes attend a Center event independently of a visit to their loved one. In a sense, life at the Center for residents' families is now less "need" driven and more "want" driven.

Today, close to 2,000 people come to our Center each month, not including the family members and friends who are visiting residents. Every day brings magical moments of connection as the elders who reside at the Scandinavian Living Center and the neighbors who participate in the Center's activities share ideas and experiences. Together they have created an "old fashioned" natural neighborhood that promotes "vibrancy for all" through meaningful connections.

Our innovative, community-centered model clearly demonstrates its capacity to energize and broaden the entire community's quality of life. Yet the principles discussed in this book cannot, and should not, be standardized.

Standardization will create built-in limitations. The development of a community center, or a cultural center, may work for one organization, but not another. A successful housing program must be creative, resourceful and integrally part of its environment, based on an understanding of and response to, the needs and wants of the whole community.

I regret that as we started to develop the Scandinavian Living Center, we did not take the time to properly research the connectional needs of the surrounding community. In other words, we didn't have a clear understanding of what kinds of connections potentially isolated populations (old and young) wanted to make with each other, and how we could seamlessly facilitate these connections. Instead of developing our Center's programs based on our constituent community's needs and desires as was done by a Norwegian community discussed in the next chapter, we created the space and hoped that we could bring groups together. Although it worked out, our development of community-centered living took much too long to implement. However, by utilizing the four principles and relying on a powerful intuition sharpened by what we had learned, we were able to facilitate beneficial interactions and thousands of human connections.

As we move forward, I am confident that, in developing the Scandinavian Living Center, we created a model that others can emulate and improve upon. It is a model formed through many connections and healthy exchanges of experiences and ideas — a model based on community-centered living.

Scandinavian Cultural Center Food Festival Connecting Friends and Neighbors

Elders come alive at the yo-yo show

*Scandinavian Living
Center Courtyard*

*Scandinavian Living Center
Single Loaded Corridor*

Scandinavian Cultural Center's Nordic Hall

CHAPTER 7

The Concepts Come Alive: From Forsmannsenteret, Norway, to Chelsea, Massachusetts

We are challenging you to participate and form an environment that suits this town's senior citizens. You can do this by expressing your expectations to the center staff. Get involved in the environment and take responsibility on how it is run. The center gives you the possibility for everyday services to the center. Every user and employee work together for this end. We challenge you to use your head and hands as you see fit. The employees and users will give of themselves to meet this end. This is not something we are doing for you. ***We want you to participate. If you do not like something, do not complain unless you are willing to participate to change it (emphasis added).***

From a brochure produced by Forsmannsenteret, an elder care center with housing in Norway: (Translated.)

62

Far too many times over the decades, I've been told that the principles of unlimited options for aging "just don't work." Even after the success of the Scandinavian Living Center, many people — inside and outside the industry — can't quite believe that the concepts of community-living, autonomy, positive residential reality and maintaining lifestyle, can readily be put into practice.

Let me introduce you to three examples of how these concepts have been put into practice.

The Formsmannsenteret Experience

"How many people does it take to start a chess club?" That was the seemingly simple question the director of Formsmannsenteret, an innovative elder care center with services, put to me. I thought I had the answer. After all, I had just spent the better of four weeks visiting sixty different facilities throughout Scandinavia. I was now sitting down with Magne Svanevik, the director of Formsmannsenteret, located in Sandefjord, Norway, which was south of Oslo on the coast of the North Sea. I was exhausted from my research and I expected to spend only about 30 minutes at the facility.

My answer was two. He replied that I was wrong. "It takes three people to start the chess club, two to play and a third to say, 'I am next.'"

The director now explained that clubs provide vital connections to the community at large. At his facility, they are very important to residents and visitors. At the time of my visit there were 36 clubs, 168 different programs, and over 245 volunteers supported by 11.25 FTEs (full-time equivalents, 1 FTE = 40 hours). Each new resident or visitor tries to find a match between his/her own special interests and those of one or more clubs. Each club provides written information about itself in a brochure, which is distributed every six months. As clubs' form or break up, that information is reported in the next six-month cycle. Moreover, each club negotiates its own separate budget with Forsmannsenteret. For example, the Whalers Association, a club at Forsmannsenteret had grown to over 200 members and had an operating budget larger than the facility itself.

Like so many aspects of Forsmannsenteret, I didn't then realize that the answer to this club question would have long lasting impact on me. Looking back, it is safe to say, my energies had been spent when I arrived in Sandefjord. Little did I realize at the time that this "brief visit," which lasted more than five hours, would be the high point of my Scandinavian research trip. It would become the model from which we would develop the new Scandinavian Living Center.

Forsmannsenteret was created in 1986 for the 55 plus adult population of Sandefjord by the municipality, but after extensive research into and a survey of their needs in relation to those of the community at large. These elements are combined with a series of programs and systems, which promote the autonomy and independence of its residents. The programs and activities help form a community center within Forsmannsenteret, making it a natural and critical link for the surrounding neighbors. Forsmannsenteret consists exclusively of private apartments with one or two rooms and balconies. (Bathrooms and kitchens are not counted as rooms.) There is an abundance of glass, flowers and paintings throughout the complex. As many as 1,000 people came through the facility during a typical day. Because of the constant need to keep abreast of new developments and prepare for continuing changes, plans for the facility are devised for only six-month periods at a time.

Only after work was completed on the Scandinavian Living Center that I realized the significance of the prior research conducted. Director Magne Svanevik explained to me that before the facility was created many issues needed to be discussed, worked out and allowed to evolve. The guiding question for their deliberation was, "Do you want people to age normally as active adults or do you want to put them in a nursing home?" The basis for Forsmannsenteret began with the premise that not all elders are sick. The municipality was influenced by research indicating that it is beneficial to age in place. But for seniors to age in place, home care needed to be established in their community. After home-care service was established, a senior center at the facility would form a link with the rest of the community.

An intensive amount of research was conducted. Researchers for the municipality found there were 7,200 people in the community with a total unemployment of six to seven percent. The same percentage of people were unemployed between ages 55 and 70 as were unemployed among people over 70 years old. Further demographic analysis showed a person's support system began to change after age 55; for example, children move away, marriages break up, a spouse passes away, or a job is lost to a younger, lower salaried person. In establishing Forsmannsenteret, the goal was to create alternative support systems for those people who encountered changes in their support networks. A report by Denmark's Commission on Aging found that the loss of social roles and functions (occupational, parental, marital, roles as friends, neighbors, etc.) are as important as biology in causing a decline in health.[28]

The municipality spent six months putting together a questionnaire and hiring five people, called "milieu workers," who would survey individuals 70 years and older and record their wants. It was important that the milieu workers not influence the seniors, but instead listen to what they said they needed. To ensure there would be no subtle influence or bias, these five individuals had no health or social service background.

Over a one-year period, the milieu workers went to over 2,700 homes. They charted a map of the city and the average age in each residential area. The survey results indicated that for most older individuals the family was no longer the basis of forming relationships with others. Better predictors of social interaction turned out to be hobbies, attitudes about culture and history (i.e., one's outlook on life), and other cooperative activities.

From the very beginning of the planning process, seniors were brought together at special meetings and asked what they wanted for themselves. The Whaling Association was one of the groups that grew out of such a meeting. The community had a proud history of whaling. In fact, most of the widows' husbands had been whale hunters. In recent years, public opinion had turned against whaling and this had decreased some local pride. The newly formed Whalers Association allowed members to socialize and discuss their thoughts and feelings about their heritage. Eventually, other interest groups also developed out of contacts made among groups of seniors who were surveyed.

Using this information, volunteers from the community began to organize into working groups. One group con-sisted of people who were good at working on a one-on-one basis. A second group was formed to coordinate interaction among groups, and a third group consisted of professionals from outside the community who would eventually serve as the professional staff for the facility and be responsible for its ongoing development. The motto for the project would be "Working together—supporting each other."

When Forsmannsenteret finally opened, its mission was clear. Every attempt would be made at Forsmannsenteret to introduce new social relations into the lives of their residents and to reinstate old roles. As a result, the seniors continue to contribute to the community and stay mentally and physically active. The residents are encouraged to take responsibility for themselves. There is no nurse at the site. "We do not want to encourage the kind of relationships which reinforce sickness," Magne Svanevik told me. Each resident decides if he or she is sick. They are educated not to wait until the last minute and told that they should know when to notify others. "If you are feeling good, come to see me. If you are feeling bad, come to see me, but do not wait until it is too late: take responsibility."

During my visit, a resident gave me a tour and explained everything offered at the facility. I saw people in their eighties working in the kitchen preparing food or washing dishes. When I asked the woman, who was giving the tour if she felt safe in an environment that encourages responsibility, she said yes. I asked her when she would see the doctor. She answered, "When I feel it is necessary." When I asked about people in need of nursing-home care, she replied, "We decide if we need to go to the nursing home. I am responsible for making that decision, and I will know when it is my time to move into a facility which offers more care."

This may not be true for people with cognitive impairments, but the important part of this statement was the strong attitude and reinforcement of a culture that empowered residents to take responsibility for their actions. Many residents may not understand this at first. This is where the staff plays a major role in the education process.

Each staff member is known as a "contact person." (Note: They are purposely not called "responsible persons" because it implies they are more responsible than the residents or volunteers.) There is a database for members' names and the clubs to which they belong. Another database consists of staff names and the members and/or residents for whom they serve as contacts. It is the resident's responsibility to talk with the contact person every six months. The contact person may remind them, but the ultimate responsibility falls on the resident. The purpose of each meeting is to develop the next six-month plan. The philosophy is to encourage total autonomy where each person has responsibility for his/her own life.

When new residents come into the center they first must have an orientation with a contact person to discuss the resident's interests. Application forms are filled out and a membership card is created. Residents are always asked what they want from the center and what they can do for the center so that everyone's skill and background can be effectively used. Currently, about one out of 10 residents volunteer to help run the center. Initially some individuals may be reluctant to discuss themselves. In all cases, they are welcome to begin the process and are repeatedly urged to join the staff member later to review their information. The application form serves as a contract between the center and the resident.

Each resident's sense of autonomy and responsibility is deeply felt. This was revealed in the story I was told of a gentleman who worked in the cafeteria at the facility. He had recently lost his wife and had a leg amputated. He worked until the day he had to go to the hospital. After recuperating from his surgery and adjusting to the loss of his wife, he insisted on returning to his work in the cafeteria.

"This is a different way of thinking, you see," Magne Svanevik told me. "It is his place and his cafeteria and he wants his place back." He also told me of a woman who used her alarm every night to summon home care before she moved into Forsmannsenteret. "Once a month she also became very sick and went to the hospital because of her asthma and heart condition. After moving to the center, she soon stopped using her alarm and after a time she only needed to go to the hospital about once a year."

My visit to Forsmannsenteret convinced me that Scandinavian eldercare philosophies and values could be implemented effectively in such a way that a housing community and its residents are situated in the present yet looking ahead to more opportunities in the future. The residents living in Forsmannsenteret are continually involved and responsible for the growth and development of their community and they remain vitally connected to the larger Sandefjord community. Forsmannsenteret has been successful because its organization incorporates the community-centered living philosophy. Residents enjoy a satisfying lifestyle with their neighbors while maintaining vital links with the community, through their service center. The Forsmannsenteret thus promotes many natural opportunities for human interactions and meaningful connections among its users. Forsmannsenteret has a slogan, "We work for friends and traditions."

For samples of the material Forsmannsenteret uses for its residents, please see the Appendix.

The Outside of Forsmannsenteret in Norway

Community Dining Area in Forsmannsenteret

Community Gift Shop at Forsmannsenteret

Barrier-busters:
Disruptors of the status quo

Dr. Bill Thomas

Shortly after the publication of ***Unlimited Options for Aging in 1995,*** Lillian Glickman, Secretary of the Executive Office of Elder Affairs in Massachusetts, invited me to speak to officials at the state level. Unknown to me at the time, Secretary Glickman also invited Dr. Bill Thomas, cofounder (with his wife Judith) of the Eden Alternative*.

The Eden Alternative is dedicated to creating quality of life for elders and their care partners, wherever they may live. Through active participation, it strives to enhance well-being by eliminating loneliness, helplessness and boredom. http://www.edenalt.org/about-the-eden-alternative[29]

As I was taking a crowded elevator to the floor of my scheduled presentation, the elevator stopped at another floor. A gentleman with shaggy hair and a beard got out, looked around, and started to say he was on the wrong floor. He jumped back in. To me it seemed odd. Finally, we reached the correct floor, I got off and I noticed this gentleman was following me. Strangely I became a little nervous. He continued to follow me into the room where I was speaking and there, I was introduced to Dr. Bill Thomas, the shaggy man behind me. I was familiar with the Eden Alternative, but this was my first introduction to Bill.

During our presentations, I discovered two important facts about Bill. First, he's a Yankee fan, and he was quick to remind me of the team's greatness. (Our discussion took place before the historic Yankee disaster/meltdown against the 2004 Boston Red Sox in the American League Championship Series.) The second, more important, fact about Bill is that he was just as upset with the institutional treatment of elders as I was.

After our presentations, we met for coffee in the cafeteria to continue our discussion. I loved Bill's presentation about the Eden Alternative, but I felt implementing this alternative in an institutional setting would only be as effective as the quality and commitment of the residence's staff. I believed that an institutional environment would seriously impede implementation of the Eden Alternative's objective. I knew Bill agreed because he went on to say that he wanted to "blow up the institutional nursing-home setting." He discussed his desire to create examples for everyone to emulate, one model at a time, letting each consumer choose his or her preferred alternative.

In 2003, Bill Thomas created the Green House Project in which nursing homes "are torn down and replaced with small home-like environments where people can live a full and interactive life." In 2005, the Robert Wood Johnson Foundation awarded him a five-year, $10 million grant to help spread the concept across the United States. http://changingaging.org/the-green-house-project/[30]

Bill's vision for the Green House Project, is divided into three areas:

Caring

- Nurtures elders in a circle of care
- Enables deep relationships between elders and caregivers
- Turns the institutional organizational chart upside down

Living

- Provides a home for 10-12 people, with private room/baths, that harmonizes with the neighboring community
- Creates a real home environment with an open kitchen, great room, and easy access to the outdoors.
- Meets federal and state licensing requirements

Thriving

- Respects flexible routines, personal preferences
- Nurtures a familial experience around a common dining table
- Welcomes friends and family members
- Encourages personal growth and enables elders to continue to pursue their interests and passions www.thegreenhouseproject.org/about/discover.[31]

Understanding and respect for each person's values and interests are important. Recognizing these differences and introducing opportunities lends itself to satisfying individual development. This is sometimes easier said than done, as was the case in my awkward reconnection with Bill Thomas.

It had been close to twenty years since we both sat down in that cafeteria to discuss the "blowing up of the nursing home industry." Over the years, I would read up on Bill and get excited about the wonderful work he was doing to change the nursing home industry through his Green House projects. And, I would follow his latest work through social media. It was a loose connection at best; I was paying attention from the sidelines. That stopped one day when I received a video clip of Bill playing the guitar and singing, I would later learn it was part of his Changing Aging Tour. Initially, I did not understand the context of the video except that he was singing and playing on stage. Looking back, I do not know why I reacted to it so strongly, but my immediate selfish reaction was why? Why are you singing and playing a guitar on stage, and not focusing on "blowing up the nursing home industry?" Singing was not your strongest gift. In fact, it became painful to listen to him and I seemed annoyed that he was trying something different — a distraction. Shame on me — the singing and playing the guitar was part of a bigger message.

As Bill went on to say, one day he saw a sign that stated, "Anyone can learn to sing" and he said to himself, "I am anyone." He had been practicing the guitar and now he would learn to sing, he would take classes for two years. Together he would practice the guitar and sing at home. And, during one of his most honest moments during this Changing Aging Tour presentation, he told everyone, "That is why I know my wife loves me" for he realized that he was "an average guitar player and not a very good singer." What mattered to Bill "was that he was able to choose." I would finally reconnect with Bill and had the opportunity to experience his entire show (twice) when the Changing Aging Tour came to the Boston area.

The takeaway for me was that community-centered living allows us to maintain our interest, our lifestyles, but it also continues the natural part of living, which is the ability to choose to try something new at any age. Bill would say, "That is how we live." Reconnecting with Bill helped reinforce in me the fact that human opportunities, at many different levels, can happen with a positive attitude and the ability to take chances, especially when you are surrounded by a caring environment that encourages living.

Bill is leading the way in influencing the redesign of an entire industry. He is accomplishing the unthinkable: the "blowing up" of the institutional nursing home setting, one facility at a time. Individual leaders, consumers and the industry are embracing the updated changes.

As of February 2015, there are 174 open Green House homes on 40 campuses in 27 states with another 186 in development.

For more information about Bill and his efforts, see: http://www.edenalt.org/ http://changingaging.org/about/

Barry Berman

Barry Berman, CEO of the Chelsea Jewish Foundation, has not only embraced the ideas of the Green House Project, but created a model to emulate. Utilizing some of Bill's ideas, Berman created a residential model nursing home that is not only appealing to residents, but welcoming to all ages.

It came about like this: On a Sunday morning, many years ago, I received a call from Barry, who wanted to know if I would join him to watch a documentary that was playing at a local movie theater. The movie featured a local young man who lived in Newton and had been diagnosed with amyotrophic lateral sclerosis (known as ALS or Lou Gehrig's disease). The movie documented the physical deterioration of a vibrant young man who was fortunate to have a family able to provide around-the-clock care and, to the extent possible, an appropriate living environment.

After the movie Barry and I went out to a local Chinese restaurant to discuss the movie. Or, so I thought. To my amazement, Barry told me he wanted to build a place that would care for young people diagnosed with ALS and multiple sclerosis (MS). Barry particularly had in mind young people whose families could not provide the needed support. He pointed out that a skilled care residence designed to support young people diagnosed with ALS did not exist. Barry wanted to build this skilled care residence in a neighborhood-like environment.

In the spring of 2007, Barry embarked on a journey to create the country's first urban Green House© skilled nursing residence — the Leonard Florence Center for Living in Chelsea, Massachusetts. In an urban setting, Barry developed a high-rise nursing home that is both welcoming and innovative. He opened the doors to residents in February 2010. By using the Green House© model of community living, Barry developed a skilled care residence that meets the needs of young adults living with ALS and MS. Today it is a model to emulate in this country and around the world.

I recently visited Barry to get an update on the impact he is having on the residents of the Leonard Florence Center for Living. During our discussion, Barry shared a story about Scott, a 60-year-old gentleman from New York diagnosed with ALS. For the past four years he had lived in an apartment with his daughter, unable to leave his bedroom because his wheelchair was too wide. In four years, he had not had a shower, only bed baths. And, he was unable to utilize the toilet, having to use a bedpan instead. Every night, Scott said two prayers before he closed his eyes. In his first prayer, Scott asked to get an acceptance phone call from Leonard Florence Center for Living. In his second prayer, Scott simply asked to die. Fortunately, Scott's first prayer came true.

When I met Scott at the Leonard Florence Center, he told me that on his first day there he asked to be left alone in the shower just so he could enjoy the sensation of water flowing down his back that had been taken away from him four years earlier. Scott went on to tell me that, since he had moved to the Center, he had been to a Celtics game and planned to attend an upcoming Red Sox game at Fenway Park. Innovative technology has enabled Scott to be more independent and live a new and dignified life. Scott is now able to open his apartment doors, turn on the lights and the television, run the elevator, and move freely through the building. My meeting with Scott, which included Scott's demonstration of the technology he uses, was amazing, but there were even more lasting memories and positive impressions to come.

Many times, during my visit to the Leonard Florence Center for Living, I heard the statement, "Until there is a cure for ALS, technology is the answer for a better life." Utilizing technology within a welcoming residential setting, even in a nursing home, is a way to encourage individuals to participate with the broader community and/or multiple human connections.

During my final moments with Barry, he mentioned two important goals. His first goal is to create the best ALS program in the world. As of this writing, Leonard Florence Center for Living is home to more people diagnosed with ALS living in one place than any other specialized care residence in the world. A state outside Massachusetts is covering the cost to convert a part of the Leonard Florence Center for Living into another ALS neighborhood for that state's residents.

Barry's second goal is just as important. Barry wants to surround residents "with the nicest and most compassionate people God has made." You cannot pay people to be nice, nor can you pay people to be disrespectful and unkind, he says.

Kindness and compassion must be natural. The perfect design and the latest technology are extremely important, but the right people will set the tone. I will add that the residential culture Barry has created — one that supports the fullest lifestyle through the commitment to autonomy and independence — sets a positive tone for the entire community.

Over the years, Barry has continued to insist that the entire nursing home industry can be changed and improved for all of us to enjoy. Barry's secret is very simple; he builds or renovates a facility based on what he would want if he had to live there, too. This philosophy should be the driving principle for all older adult housing. It should become a movement defined by the new consumers — all of us, as we age.

After our visit, as I was leaving, Barry asked if I wanted to take the food I was eating with me. Thrilled with this prospect, it dawned on me: when was the last time I walked out of a nursing home happy that they had offered me food?

A few weeks later Barry invited me to the Boston premiere of "Trans Fatty Lives," a film by Patrick Sean O'Brien, a resident of the Leonard Florence Center for Living since 2010. A winner of the Audience Award for Best Documentary at the Tribeca Film Festival, this powerful film captures Patrick's remarkable life after he was diagnosed with ALS at the age of 30. To my surprise, at the end of the movie, I ran into Scott and his daughter in the lobby. I discovered the impact of Barry's work from a simple statement made by another gentleman standing by Scott. As he was leaving us, he said to Scott, "I'll see you back at the house." This was a very simple and extraordinarily transformational statement in that the nursing home Barry had built for people with ALS had become their house too.

When Leornard Florence had opened, Barry had asked me if this was what I was looking for in nursing home care.

I remember thinking that what I was truly looking for were more people like Barry who could help transform entire institutional living approaches. As heroes do, Barry leads by inspiring others to think outside the box and overcome any obstacles in their way. He keeps it very simple, and that is the secret to success.

To learn more about Barry Berman and to support his many innovative ideas please go to: http://www.chelsea jewish.org/senior-living-and-short-term-rehabilitation/ long-term-rehabilitation/skilled-nursing-care-green-house-chelsea/

———

Ordinary people can do extraordinary things. A passion for change and a now willing society are making it easier to transform inadequate, outdated housing for an aging population. These examples, along with work that is being done by others, are a call to action toward enhancement in housing options that offer dignified connections to others. Through places like Forsmannsenteret, and people like Barry Berman and Bill Thomas, the nursing home — once thought of as the most institutionalized living setting — is removing aspects of institutional living and moving toward more dignified human connections.

Leonard Florence Center for Living Entrance

Leonard Florence Center for Living Common Area

Leonard Florence Center for Living Elevator Lobby

CHAPTER 8

A Call to Action

Fifty percent of the population is smarter than me;
the other fifty percent does not know it yet

did not read about community-centered living, I observed
it in Scandinavia. No one told me about the connection to
the surrounding community; it was subtle, natural, and I
experienced it. The human connections and observations in
Scandinavia stayed with me and it had a meaningful impact
on me. Community-centered living is something everyone
can do.

When we decide to separate our elders or any age group,
we stop the human connections that need to take place in
all our personal journeys. It can be a potential loss for many
generations. This was reinforced when I was speaking to a
friend. She told me about a conversation she had with her
son concerning the most important person in his life. It was
not his parents or grandparents, but the person that connected and introduced his grandparents. It was someone he

will never know or meet, but he made a difference in his life. This human interaction impacted her son and will continue to impact future generations. This simple story is a powerful illustration of the impact community centered living can have for many generations.

This book *Creating Unlimited Options for Aging* was written for consumers. Through consumers, an entire elder care and a housing industry can change. Sometimes the industry leaders do not listen, but consumers do. Simply bringing people into a community centered living facility to gather and interact, encourages observation and understanding of the importance of human connections. The housing industry is made up of industry leaders and these leaders are also consumers that need to be reeducated and connected to the importance and impact of community centered living. The more people that are exposed and allowed to observe the community centered living philosophy, the more they will start to demand it. At a recent city building meeting concerning the development of a new assisted living facility in Newton, Massachusetts, the neighbors and the politicians asked the developer if they were going to build space for the community like the "Scandinavian Living Center," according to what I was later told. Sadly, it became part of the negotiating instead of part of the discussion on how the developer could better integrate a new facility into the fabric of the community.

Beyond the obvious human interaction that takes place within an environment that allows community-centered living, there will always be an opportunity for an exchange of ideas and observations. Through these educating interactions, different types of options can develop and be passed on to other people. In a sense, the principles discussed in this book can be used as a catalyst for fulfilling the needs of diverse groups of individuals. Copying, emulating and improving upon can be results of these human interactions and observations.

To facilitate lasting change in all types of long-term-care housing, providers need re-educating. However, equally important is the education of the user. As potential users themselves, people must realize that their individual beliefs determine their perception of reality and influence their actions. People must realize that they are the agents most responsible for what happens to them now and in the future. As future users of the elder-care infrastructure, we must not limit our own options. Our beliefs and expectations for aging need to be more positive. We must acknowledge that we have unlimited options.

Elders should not lose the autonomy enjoyed through-out youth. They can retain their power and enthusiasm and be responsible for their later years. Although the solution and answers will vary tremendously with everyone, the ideal should be a lifestyle that the young will envy and anticipate. "I wake with expectations and go to bed with experiences. Life is an adventure for better or for worse. But it should not be lived passively: I can influence it myself."[32]

Mats Thorslund, Ph.D., has an apt metaphor for making cosmetic changes in outdated institutional housing communi-ties: "If you fall off a skyscraper, halfway down everything still works. Then you hit the ground." Right now, our outdated insti-tutional communities are halfway down. Changing wallpaper, installing new carpeting or creating an exclusive country club-like environment with all the frills, but isolated from the rest of the community, is not the answer. More basic changes must occur. We will demand a welcoming residential setting, which maintains our lifestyle and autonomy while being connected to the entire community. Anything less will not be "practical."

Greater involvement in the community is important to the future of the elder-housing industry, but it must have local roots. Every facility in Scandinavia either has a program or is planning such programs to bring people into their communities, such as common dining rooms, adult gyms, etc. Unfortunately, in the United States only a fraction of elder housing, such as the Scandinavian Living Center, have any genuine connections with the community.

An abundance of research supports the concepts discussed in this book. I am convinced that many of these common-sense ideas and practices can work. The industry must usher in a new generation of American communities that truly serve the entire population. People do not want to be in an isolated environment without choices. People want to be independent and in control, free to develop and grow as they see fit.

Every residential housing setting must become a place that energizes the community and its residents. The concepts discussed here cannot and should not be standardized. Standardization will create built-in limitations. The development of a community center, for instance, may work for one organization, but not for another. A good community must be creative, resourceful and a vital part of its environment.

When I was a young man, my father handed me a book about the history of Italy. My father was born in 1920 and grew up in Southern Italy until he was twelve. There were no words except, "You might find this interesting." As I read through the book I discovered that Italians from southern Italy during the early part of the 20th century were treated worse than black slaves before the Civil War. In fact, the book explained why education was precious to my father; southern Italians were denied the best education and they were looked down upon by the Italians in the north. Reading through those pages it became clear why my father with a fourth-grade education needed to self-educate himself and why he preached the importance of a good education to all his children. His work ethic and discipline stemmed from his need to take control of his life and not allow others to dictate his fate. Without sitting down to explain how life had impacted him and why his love for this country was so strong, he simply shared a book.

Taking a page from my father's example, I ask you to simply share this book with friends and family if you cannot find the words or feel uncomfortable discussing aging. For the rest of you, I ask that you begin to create unlimited options for aging and that you find a way to do it better. Give us an example to observe, and give us an example to improve upon.

When we, working with any age group, conceptualize individuals as persons, we give them access to their strengths. If they do not have to fight the environment, negative labeling, or the isolating obstacles society creates, then we have freed them to express and enjoy their unique personhood. When we can connect in a natural and healthy setting, we are given access to potential wisdom and concepts, helping us create unlimited options for aging.

For More Information

Please contact Joe Carella at the Scandinavian Living Center, 206 Waltham St. West Newton, MA 02465 or via email at joe@slcenter.org

The Scandinavian Living Center offers seniors innovative assisted living, where community, culture and comfort come together. There is a multitude of rich and varied cultural activities for residents, family members and the community-at-large to enjoy. To expand our offerings, the Scandinavian Cultural Center was created in 2012 under the guidance of a Cultural Director. We have been proud to present notable art exhibits, theatrical and musical performances, highly regarded speakers, noteworthy lectures, popular movies, and fun and light-hearted children's programs. Most events are held in our bright and beautiful Nordic Hall, which can accommodate 125 guests and is equipped with a state-of-the-art audio-visual system.

The Nordic Hall also provides a meeting place for many organizations in the area, enabling residents to continue life-long hobbies and pursuits as well as maintain contact with old friends and the broader community. For example, a group comes to the Center through the Newton Parks and Recreation Department each week to play cards and socialize for the afternoon; other professional and outside groups use the hall for meetings, seminars and workshops. Many opportunities for enjoyment and engagement can be found right here.

Over 2,000 people visit the Scandinavian Living Center every month to participate in our activities. Each Saturday, the Kaffestugan (café) is staffed by volunteers serving a variety of sandwiches, desserts and refreshments. It is a way for people from the community to come in and socialize. The residents of the SLC never feel isolated, as there is always a sense of vibrancy around them and a flurry of visitors within their surroundings.

Our goals are twofold. We seek to be a destination for residents, their neighbors and friends in the community to enjoy stimulating events and we strive to carry out our vital mission: to provide affordable housing and assistance to elders and to support cultural enrichment and community connections. Our success is based on the belief that "age does not limit one's personhood."

Exhibit A

Forsmannsenteret
Sandefjord
kommune

Arbeidslag

Ledelse
(Leader)

Ansatte
(Staff)

Identifikasjon
(Identification)

Frivillig arbedslag
(Volunteers)

Brukere
(Users)

Triangular diagram depicting the importance of the Users.

Exhibit B

Application for User Card

Please answer the questions on this application, either by yourself or with help from one of the employees at the center, so we can give you a User card. All information is confidential.

Name: _____ Date of Birth: _____

Address: _____

Tel: _____ Married: ____ Live Alone: _____ Other: _____

Which center do you plan to use?

Bugarden ___ Frammaes ___ Forsmannsenteret ___ Solvang

Next of Kin: (Family, neighbor, friend who will know if you are sick, on vacation, etc.)

Name: _____

Address: _____

Tel. Home: _____ Tel. Work: _____

Relation to you: _____

What are your hobbies, "wishes and dreams?" _____

Which service do you plan to use? (underline or mark with x)

Hairdresser, Foot Doctor (Foot Therapist), Food Service, Library, Interest Groups, Clubs, Courses (educational), Meetings/Activities

Do you want to help run the center as a volunteer? _____

Date: _____ Staff member (in conversation with): _____

Sandefjord County

Exhibit C

Welcome to a User Conversation

A *User* conversation is a meeting between you and an employee of the center. We explain about the possibilities at the Center for Elders, how it is operated, register your name and address, and talk to you about your interests and wishes.

We agree on how you will use the center, if you want tasks at the center, or whether the staff shall work with you in different settings. At the same time, the staff gets to know what you feel the center should offer. After you have had a *User* conversation a *User* card will be given to you.

What is a *User* card?

A *User* card is a plastic ID card that gives you entrance and lets you take part in the offerings at the center. Registration as a *User* is necessary for several reasons:

1. We want to keep track of which center you prefer to use.

2. We would like to send you information about the center's offerings, activities and programs.

3. If a regular *User* does not show up for some time we would like to find out if it is because of sickness or some other reason.

4. It allows us to refuse or exclude those individuals who are not eligible.

5. We can invite you to *User* meetings.

User Cards are free.

We welcome you as a *User* of the Center for Elders.

Exhibit D

User Special Liability Form

Name: _____ User No.: _____

Address: _____ Tel. No.: _____

Agreement: Type of Work/Responsibility _____

Weekdays: _____

From (time/start): _____ to (time/end): _____

Food (reimbursement offer): _____

Transportation: _____

Agreement valid from: _____

Next time (we will talk again): _____

Contact person at the center: _____

Group: _____ (i.e., which group does contact person belong to)

Contact person for group/club: _____

Follow-up and continuous education needed: _____

Exhibit E

Oath of Silence

I understand:

> that I in my volunteer work might come across personal information regarding the individuals that should not be known by outsiders;

> that this work requires responsibilities, loyalty, and respect for the individual's right to protection against unlawful or harmful use of personal information.

I promise:

> not to give any personal information to anyone except those who have the right to such information regarding their work.

I understand:

> that my oath of silence is in effect after I have terminated this volunteer work.

Name: _____

Place: _____ Date: _____

About the Author

Joe Carella is the Executive Director of the Scandinavian Charitable Society of Greater Boston. The design and development of the Scandinavian Living Center in Newton, Massachusetts, is based on the research and principles from *Unlimited Options for Aging*. He has shared these concepts on a national stage.

Joe has an MBA from Babson College and an undergraduate degree from Northeastern University. He was a founding board member of the Newton Cultural Alliance, which supports the performing and visual arts in the Newton and Boston area. He also serves on the board of Elizabeth Seton and Marillac Residence, Inc., two nonprofit elder care organizations in Wellesley, Massachusetts. Joe lives in Bedford, Massachusetts, with his wife, Carole, and three children.

References

1. US Department of Health and Human Services, Administration for Community Living. Website access 18 April 2016. http://www.aoa.acl.gov/aging_statistics/ future_growth/future_growth.aspx#gender

2. US Department of Health and Human Services, National Institute on Aging. Website access 18 April 2016. https:// www.nia.nih.gov/research/publication/global-health- and-aging/humanitys-aging

3. Hopcke, Robert H. *There Are no Accidents: Synchronicity and the Stories of Our Lives.* Riverhead Books, New York, NY, 1997.

4. Gross, Ronald, Gross, Beatrice, Seidman, Sylvia, eds. *The New Old: Struggling for Decent Aging.* Anchor Press/ Doubleday, New York, 1978.

5. Frerickson, Barbara L. *Love 2.0; How our supreme emotion Affects Everything We Feel, Think, Do, And Become.* Penguin Group, New York, NY 2013.

6. Proctor, Bob. *The Art of Living.* Tarcher/Penguin Books, New York, NY, 2015.

7. Bowker, Lee H. *Humanizing Institutions for the Aged.* D. C. Heath and Company, Lexington, MA, 1982, pp. 9-14.

8. Langer, Ellen J.& Abelson, Robert P. "A Patient by Any Other Name: Clinician Group Difference in Labeling Bias," *Journal of Consulting and Clinical Psychology*, 1974, No. 1, pp. 4-9.

9. Lefcourt, H. "The Function of the Illusion of Control and Freedom," *American Psychologist*, 1973, 28, pp. 417- 425.

10. Langer, Ellen J. & Rodin, Judith. "The Effects of Choice and Enhanced Personal Responsibility for the Aged: A Field Experiment in an Institutional Setting," *Journal of Personality and Social Psychology*, 1976, Vol. 34. pp. 191-198

11. Lawton, Powell M., Newcomer, Robert J. & Byerts, Thomas 0., eds. *Community Planning for an Aging Society*, Dowden, Hutchinson & Ross, Inc. Stroudsburg, PA,1976, pp. 36 and 167.

12. Pastalan, Lean, A. & Carson, Daniel, H., eds. *Spatial Behavior of Older People*, University of Michigan. Ann Arbor, Michigan, 1970.

13. Proshansky, H.M., Ittleson, W.H., & Rivlin, LOG., eds. *Environmental Psychology: Man and His Physical Setting*, New York, Holt Reinhart and Winston, Inc., 1970.

14. Firestone, Ira J, Lichtman, Gary M.& Evans, John R. "Privacy and Solidarity: Effects of Nursing Home Accommodation on Environmental Perception and Sociability Preferences,"

International Journal of Aging and Human Development, Vol. 11(3), 1980, pp. 229-241.

15. Rodin, Judith & Langer, Ellen J. "Long-Term Effects of a Control-Relevant Intervention with the Institutionalized Aged," *Journal of Personality and Social Psychology,* 1977, Vol. 35, No. 12. pp. 897-902

16. Pedersen, Jorgen B. "Attitudes to Aging and Old Age" *Danish Medical Bulletin, Journal of the Health Sciences,* No. 3, Vol. 39, June, 1992. pp. 213-215.

17. Langer, Ellen J. & Benevento, Anne. "Self-Induced Dependence," *Journal of Personality and Social Psychology,* 1978, Vol. 36, No. 8. pp. 886-893.

18. Rodin, Judith & Langer, Ellen J. "Aging Labels: The Decline of Control and the Fall of Self-Esteem," *Journal of Social Issues,* 1980, Vol. 36, No. 2, pp.12-29.

19. Langer, Ellen J.& Abelson, Robert P. "A Patient by Any Other Name: Clinician Group Difference in Labeling Bias," *Journal of Consulting and Clinical Psychology,* 1974, No. 1, pp. 4-9.

20. Langer, Ellen J. & Benevento, Anne. "Self-Induced Dependence," *Journal of Personality and Social Psychology,* 1978, Vol. 36, No. 8. pp. 886-893.

21. Rodin, Judith & Langer, Ellen J. "Aging Labels: The Decline of Control and the Fall of Self-Esteem," *Journal of Social Issues,* 1980, Vol. 36, No. 2, pp.12-29.

22. Chopra, Deepak. *Ageless Body, Timeless Mind,* Harmony Books, New York, 1993.

23. Lewis, Myrna. "Feelings," *New Choices,* June,1993, p. 92.

24. Kirk, Henning. "Images of Aging—over the Last 100 Years," *Danish Medical Bulletin, Journal of the Health Sciences*, No. 3, Vol. 39, June 1992. pp. 202-203.

25. Day, Davis, Dove and French. *Journal of Advertising Research*, "Reaching The Senior Citizen Market(s)," Dec., 1987/Jan., 1988, p. 27.

26. Pallesen, Axel, E. "Care for the Dying in Denmark," *Danish Medical Bulletin, Journal of the Health Sciences*, No. 3, Vol. 39, June, 1992, pp. 253-255.

27. Mattiasson, Anne-Catherine & Andersson, Lars. "Elderly Patients' Satisfaction with Nursing Home Care." Paper presented at XVth Congress of International Association of Gerontology, Budapest, Hungary, July 7, 1993.

28. Kahler, Margrethe. "Ten Years after the Commission on Aging—Ideas and Results," *Danish Medical Bulletin, Journal of the Health Sciences*, No. 3, Vol. 39, June, 1992. pp. 216, 277.

29. About Eden Alternative* http://www.edenalt.org/about-the-eden-alternative

30. Changing Aging with Dr. Bill Thomas, http://changing aging.org/the-green-house-project/

31. The Green House Project; "caring homes for meaningful lives" www.thegreenhouseproject.org/about/discover.

32. Moller, Esther. "Being Old" *Danish Medical Bulletin, Journal of the Health Sciences*, No. 3, Vol. 39, June, 1992. p. 201.